The

# NAKED TRUTH

—————— of a ——————

# HEALER

*The Path to My Authentic Self*

Émilie Macas

Tellwell Talent
www.tellwell.ca

ISBN
978-0-2288-7380-8 (Hardcover)
978-0-2288-7379-2 (Paperback)
978-0-2288-7381-5 (eBook)

# Table of Contents

# Part II

*From My Heart to Yours*

# Dedication

To my husband and my beautiful children. You are my inspiration; you are the breath and the light of my life.

*Ma petite maman*, my shining star: *Je t'aime comme tout l'univers et plus encore.*

To my Anais: I hope this book will bring you healing as well.

To my father: may peace surround your heart.

# Disclaimer

This book reflects the author's recollection and memories of facts, and the most impactful moments of her life.

Names of individuals were changed to protect and respect their privacy. Some places and events were condensed and modified for literary effect. Some dialogues were recreated.

The author shares a deep reflection on her healing journey. The information provided is not intended and should not be construed as medical advice, nor is it a substitute for professional medical expertise or treatment.

The reader should consult a physician in matters relating to his/her/their health.

# PART I

## WHEN IT ALL BEGAN

# THE MAN WITH THE BELT

It burned so much. I thought I might be bleeding. No, wait . . . I *was* bleeding.

My legs were shaking, and my entire little body trembled uncontrollably. I felt like I was about to collapse. I could feel the coldness of his heart as he doubled up his Portuguese army belt to make sure it was painful enough. I thought, *Why is he doing this to me? Why is he doing this to* us? *Why do we need to feel pain to teach us discipline?*

As he struck me with his belt, I suddenly noticed a numbness in my body. One after the other, hit after hit, I started to get used to the excruciating pain of each succeeding blow. The real pain, though, was the unbearable pain in my chest. It was suffocating. My heart was shattered, my love destroyed. Papa, you broke my heart.

Why did you want to hurt us? How could the superhero I needed to protect us from harm be the villain in disguise? Are you not supposed to love us, cherish us, and protect us from harm?

This man was my father, but I could not recognize him. The father I knew was respected, cultured, and admired. He was handsome, tall, and well built. He had profound brown eyes and thick, wavy, dark hair. He took pride in his appearance and made sure to take care of himself. He took pride in the fact that many people thought he was a doctor or an engineer. People always commented on how well he maintained his physical appearance, and how well he articulated himself. He had a daily ritual where he would spend a good hour cleaning his hands and scrubbing underneath his fingernails after a long hot shower. He left no trace that he was actually a construction worker. The man before me was my father, but he was also the torment of my upbringing.

As he towered over me and my ten-year-old sister, his face turned dark. I had always remembered his hands to be soft from all the self-care moisturizing he did. But that was before he brought out his army belt from the wardrobe. He embraced the texture of his army belt with his tough construction-working hands.

I tried to understand why he was hurting me. I was so confused, and my head was spinning. His belt was rough like a rope. With each pause between hits, my legs agonized and blistered with pain from the friction burns.

I heard my sister start to sob in pain. He whipped his belt at us both at the same time. The pain resonated up my legs like a bell struck each hour. From the corner of my teary eyes, I could see my mother watching. Her body trembled at the sight of each blow with a fear that completely petrified her. She appeared as still as stone.

All of this happened way too fast. My family and I lived in a two-bedroom apartment in a three-storey building in Chambéry, France, the city where I was born. Every evening at eight p.m. we would watch the news in the living room while we ate our dinner.

My older sister Anais was upset with my mother that day. She had asked once again if she could participate with her class on a school field trip, where they would leave early in the morning and return around five p.m. She never had the experience to participate in anything. The answer was always no.

My mother, sister, and I were washing and drying the dishes as part of our after-dinner routine. My mother was short with a well-pronounced, curvy body. She had short, thinning brown hair, and had soft and clear skin. In contrast to my father, my mother did not care about her appearance. My mother worked as a cleaning lady. She wore clothing that was donated to her by her clients. Her time was always limited, and so was her energy. She appeared ten years older than her age. My mother lived with depression, and anyone could feel her sadness just by looking at her melancholic, delicate, and tired hazel eyes, but at the same time she had an incredibly strong will, and she would never give up. Everyone would compliment my mother on how beautiful she was, especially when she first arrived in France as a Portuguese immigrant in the late 1960s. She was still beautiful in my eyes, but her sadness masked it. When Anais was drying the last set of dishes, she tried one last time to convince my mother to participate in the class field trip.

"Well, tonight I will not kiss you goodnight," Anais said to her in frustration, wiping down a plate and placing it inside the cupboard.

Every morning and every night, Anais and I would kiss our parents before we left the house for school, or before we went to bed. We both felt emotionally disconnected from them, but it was respectful, and we were taught to do this gesture at a very young age. It was also the only time we received any bit of affection from our parents.

What Anais didn't know was that my father had been drawing nearer to the kitchen and had heard her say these words to my mother. Before entering the kitchen, he made his way to his bedroom to grab his Portuguese army belt. When he came to the kitchen, he was ready to attack.

"Who do you think you are to answer to your mother this way?" my father shouted as he grabbed Anais's arm with a firm grip, holding his army belt in his dominant hand.

"Tonight you will learn what respect and discipline means. It seems you do not have a clear idea. So let me show you what discipline means."

My mother, who was cleaning the sink, turned around in disbelief and dropped her cleaning towel on the floor.

"Antonio! Antonio! What are you doing? What are you doing?" my mother exclaimed.

"*Turn around and face the wall!*" my father shouted at my sister, ignoring my mother's cries as he led Anais to face the wall where our kitchen table was.

I was trying to grasp what was happening in front of my eyes, but it made no sense. I saw my father double his belt as my sister stood facing the wall, her body shivering in fear. Something came over me. As he raised his arm to launch the first hit, I ran between them and jumped toward him to intercept his attack.

"*No papa! No papa!* You are not going to hurt her. Please don't do that!" I shouted at him, begging while holding tightly to his legs. He pushed me aside. Enraged, he grabbed me and shoved my face to the wall so I could stand beside my sister.

"*You want to cry too? Tonight you and Anais will learn what discipline means and who is the authority in this house! You will cry together!*"

That's when it began. The pain, the bleeding, the crying, the fear. I can still hear the echoes of the belt cracking in our tiny apartment kitchen.

My mother had always preferred to hide things from my father. She normally did not go against his ways. But that day, I saw her bravely and with great strength stand up to my father.

"Antonio, please. Please stop. Antonio, enough! Stop it! It is enough!"

My father only stopped when he thought it was enough. She tried to stop him. She did her best. Her voice was hoarse and shaken as she begged him to stop. Under this tyrannous roof, no voice other than his could be heard.

I reached out for my sister. We held hands tightly until it was all over. When he'd had enough, he sent us to bed. By that time, my mother had clasped her hands over her eyes in disbelief, tears dropping from her face. He did not even allow my mother to wish us goodnight or visit us in our bedroom to check in on us.

I went to the bathroom, and when I tried to sit on the toilet my tears erupted. The pain on my legs was so intense I couldn't sit straight to pee. I watched my sister clench her teeth as she tried to do the same when I was done. We got ourselves a facecloth and, with cold water, gently tapped on each other's sore legs to alleviate the pain.

"Next time don't say anything. Stay quiet. If you didn't say anything to him, he wouldn't have hurt you. He was mad at me, not you. I don't want him to do to you what he has done to me before." My sister hugged me tightly, whispering these words in my ears as she cried.

"What do you mean?" I asked. "He used to hit you when you were younger?"

"Yes, Émilie. Papa used to hit me often when I was little. He would have fits and he would hit me. I know he slapped Maman too. This is why I am so scared of him, and I only feel at peace when he is not at home. I am afraid, and I can't breathe when he is here. I never know what can be said or done that will make him upset. I am always scared for you. You are not quiet, and you always have the answer at the tip of your tongue. You know he does not like that. See? Today he hurt you too. Promise me not to do that again. Promise!"

I walked out of the bathroom and slowly dragged my feet across the hallway toward my bedroom. I sat on my bed for a moment, but the back of my knees agonized in pain as soon as they rested on the comforter. I lay in my bed uncomfortably, trying to find a position that would not hurt my little legs, and gazed at the dark ceiling. I understood that she had experienced this behaviour before. She had been beaten in the past. Little did I know, long after the scars of my legs healed, I would carry the wounds of hurt in my heart.

I thought about what my sister said to me in the bathroom, but I couldn't make that promise. That day, I realized that my father was not the person I thought he was. I felt that my entire world had been shattered, my heart ripped out of my chest. I knew that I would never stay quiet. I couldn't.

From that day forward, I took on the role of the superhero in my family. I became the protector I never had. I promised myself that I would always defend my mom and my sister. I would rescue them from him. I knew that I would face him again. The day I made this promise to myself, I was four years old.

# THE DOUBLE LIFE OF A PREACHER

Being disciplined, educated, were qualities ingrained in our everyday lives. We were expected to perform exceptionally well in school. And when I say exceptionally well, I mean that we were expected to be at the top of our class. Second place was not acceptable for my father, and neither was scoring a grade lower than 100 percent. In France, each elementary school subject was graded out of twenty, and each subject was added to make a total of 100 percent.

I remember my second-grade year, when I was attending a private school. At that time, this was something rare for the children of immigrants. That year, I had been experiencing the unacceptance and alienation of racism. A group of kids believed that I had no right to be in their school because my parents were immigrants. Every time my mother would go to my school she was avoided like a plague. These parents taught their children not to play with me. Every day for months, I was ridiculed, mocked, and marginalized, but I refused to let them affect my focus. I made sure to pack these hurtful comments deep inside of me. They echoed my father's words and they added to the belief that I was not good enough. But my need to be seen and validated by my father was stronger, so I worked extra hard to keep my grades high.

Close to the end of spring, I was sitting with a little boy who was tied with me for top of the class. The day we received our report cards, I waited eagerly for my father to come home and finish his daily shower and self-care ritual. He came to the kitchen and, as proud as I was, I handed him my report card. I had scored 96.5 percent for my final average. My little chest filled with pride, excitement, and joy, and I could not wait to see the happiness on his face at seeing my grades.

"Papa, you are going to be so proud. I did so well, just like you wanted," I said to him as I watched him open the envelope.

I couldn't wait for him to make eye contact with me. He leaned against the kitchen counter and calmly read my report card. He finally made eye contact and gave me a smile.

"Good work, Émilie, but it could have been better. It is still not 100 percent," he said calmly. He set the report card back on the counter, tapped the top of my head, and walked away.

These words sank in my stomach. I could feel my heart race and my neck start to sweat. I was devastated. I ran to my bedroom and cried. He was not proud of me. He did not even acknowledge my accomplishment. He dismissed me, invalidated me. It was not good enough. I felt invisible. When was I ever going to be enough for my father?

My father was born in the mid-1940s in a rural town located in the southern region of Portugal. While growing up, he lived in a tiny white house made of adobe brick. The roof was made of old clay tiles, and inside the house the floor was made of dirt. He lived with his parents, his older brother John, and his two sisters Aurora and Linda. His parents were very poor, and they would cultivate their small land to grow food. His father, who worked as a labourer in construction, was the sole provider of the family. His family suffered from famine, and they had very little food to divide between them. With the food shortage during the Second World War, my father and his family ate divided portions of bread, olive oil, and olives.

At the age of six, my father was forced to work in construction. He worked long hours. At home he slept on a bed made of straw and shared a bedroom with his siblings. Education was a luxury for him since basic education in Portugal was offered until the fourth grade. My father completed night classes until he finished basic schooling. He always had the ambition to become educated and work for himself one day. He wanted to outgrow his impoverished life and make a better living for himself. I understood that he never had a choice in his upbringing. He did not have a regular, normal childhood. His circumstances dictated his reality as a child. In his eyes, Anais and I were extremely privileged to have the opportunity to go to school. It was our duty to excel in all levels. He expected us to be perfect, academically speaking; responsible for our household chores; extremely polite; and obedient. We had to strive to meet his standards of perfection and nothing less.

Cleanliness and tidiness were mandatory at home. Before leaving for school, we had to clean up after ourselves after breakfast. We weren't allowed to leave the dishes to dry in the dishrack. We had to wash the dishes, dry them, and put them back in the cupboard. When we made our beds, we had to make sure that the top sheets were tucked in underneath the mattress, and we combed out any visible wrinkles on the pillows and comforter. Since our schools were only a ten-minute walk from our apartment, we would come home for lunch and repeat the process to keep our kitchen spotless. After school, we were expected to not only do our homework, but also keep up with the cleaning demands of the house. We had to make sure there was not a single speck of dust on the furniture or the baseboards, because when my father would come home the first thing, he would do was inspect our apartment to ensure all was spotless.

My father had an interesting connection—or disconnection, you might say—with religion. He strongly opposed the Catholic faith and was against priests, but I never understood why. My mother, on the other hand, was born and raised in a devout Catholic household. During my mother's upbringing, my mother and grandmother would attend Mass every Sunday. When I was two years old, my father started studying the Bible with the Jehovah's Witnesses. After a few months of Bible study, my father immersed himself in the Jehovah's

Witness philosophy. Against my mother's will, we too were forced to follow my father's footsteps and attend the Jehovah's Witness meetings.

According to the Jehovah's Witnesses worldview, only Jehovah's followers are chosen to live in God's kingdom on earth after Armageddon. If you want to be spared by God and live on Paradise Earth, you must follow Jehovah's law as dictated in the Bible and follow the Watch Tower Society founded by Charles Russell. Followers of Jehovah believe that they are the chosen ones, while the rest of society is under Satan's influence. Jehovah's Witnesses don't believe in celebrating Christmas, Easter, birthdays, or any national holidays. They are also taught to oppose blood transfusions. Even if a loved one was at the brink of death, the family was forbidden under Jehovah's law to accept a blood transfusion, even if it could save that life.

They also limit their interactions with the worldly. The "worldly" referred to those who were not within the Jehovah's Witness faith, or those who were non-believers. I heard of cases where parents of the Jehovah's Witness faith would shun their children, who later in life decided that they no longer wanted to practice the Jehovah's Witness faith anymore. As such, Jehovah's Witnesses avoid associating with the worldly because they do not want to be tempted.

As a child, I never had a birthday, a Christmas, or an Easter celebration. And even though my mother never embraced the Jehovah's Witness faith, my father forbade her to practice hers. Despite being Catholic, she was not allowed to celebrate any holiday or religious festival. When my classmates would talk about their birthdays at school, it was hurtful to hear about what their parents did for them to celebrate their special day. My birthday was treated like any other day at home. My father never acknowledged the day, nor did he do anything special. My mother would wish me happy birthday and buy me a single pastry, but she would hide it and make me eat it in a hurry. The fear that my father could show up at any time gave us chills down our spines. Everything was hidden from my father, and it felt like we were committing a crime for such simple and innocent gestures.

Christmases were also very sad for me. Not because of the lack of gifts, but because of how distant my family was during the holidays. I felt like I had nothing in common to share with my classmates. We would all return from Christmas break, and while they would talk about their gifts and their family, I would have a holiday that was just treated as any ordinary day. No togetherness with family or friends. No gifts. Just another holiday that it was forbidden to acknowledge. It made me feel so unseen, so unheard, so insignificant.

Jehovah's Witnesses would undertake the responsibility to save non-believers by attempting to convert them. They believed that by preaching door to door, they were trying to convert others into their faith so they too could have a chance to be spared when God returned for the final judgement.

At the Jehovah's Witnesses meetings, men were expected to dress in a suit and tie, while women dressed modestly in a dress or a skirt that fell below the knee. I liked wearing dresses to the meetings, and my mother took pleasure in sprucing up her young girls for the occasion as well.

When we attended the weekly meetings, my butt ached from sitting on the seats for so long, but I tried so hard not to fidget. I really wanted Jehovah to be proud of me. And I didn't want to anger my father in front of the other preachers, either.

At home, we prayed together before each meal, and at night individually before going to bed. I was grateful for my relationship with the Creator, and I cherished my connection with Him. My mother would practice prayer with me and always encouraged us to practice gratitude. I knew my mother did not refer to God as Jehovah, but I was much more in tune with knowing that they were the same God. Without being able to explain this, I knew in my little heart that God was one, God was love, and God was non-judgment. I did not fear God, even though I was taught at a young age that He was going to kill everyone who did not comply with His rules. Somehow, I had a hard time comprehending that if we were all His children, then how could He just select who was worthy of life and who deserved death? All of this never made any clear sense to me.

My father raised us to be perfect, but I learned to pay close attention to my father's actions, and I realized he was demanding something from us that was humanly impossible, because no one is perfect, especially him. My father was emotionally disconnected from us and running a dictatorship. My sister and I never experienced compassion from him or saw him as a loving husband to our mother. We were raised to fear him, to be his slaves and not question anything. My poor sister, being the oldest, was used to his physical abuse. If my father would call her name out loud, she would urinate herself in fear.

After a year of his Bible study with the Jehovah's Witnesses, my father became baptized and converted completely in the Jehovah's faith. He was ambitious and saw opportunities to grow and have more status and responsibility in the congregation. He was thirsty for any form of power. My father loved to show off to the brothers and sisters that he was a loving father, and a devoted husband to a wife who was worldly. They pitied my mother and felt sorry for my father, because he was raising two daughters alone in the Jehovah's Witnesses faith. From time to time my father would show off his financial status, and make it known to the congregation that he would give large donations by cheque so he would be recognized for his generosity.

My mother was a personal support worker for a wealthy older gentleman whom we referred to as "Papi." She loved working with seniors. She had a tremendous amount of love and patience for them.

"Émilie, children and babies have more opportunities to be adopted or taken care of by society, whereas elderly people are always forgotten about," she once said to me.

My mother lost her father from a sudden cardiac arrest when she was only five years old. Papi became a father figure for her. She loved and cared for him deeply. She cooked meals for him, bathed him, walked with him, helped him with his bicycle exercises, washed and ironed his laundry, and cleaned his house. When he went to the hospital for routine procedures or for a surgery, he wouldn't even allow the nurses to clean him. He always requested my mother be the one to care for him.

My mother worked long hours as a cleaning lady. There were some days when she would clean offices at night and be home after ten p.m. Sometimes she would prepare lunch for us for the following day. If she was too tired to prepare lunch that night, she would wake up early the following morning. On average, she would work about fourteen to fifteen hours a day, surpassing my father's days most of the time. Her life was not easy. She looked exhausted, but I was too young to understand the many faces of depression.

My mother was born in Lisbon in the early 1940s. Her father had earned a decent living for himself, but after his death my grandmother struggled to pay the bills and sustain their apartment. Like my father, my mother grew up poor and did not have a lot to eat. With Portugal being a small poor country under a dictatorship during and after the Second World War, both my parents had a challenging upbringing with poverty and a lack of carefreeness in their childhood.

My mother took pride in dressing her daughters up like little princesses. She saved a lot of her earnings to shop for dresses and clothing at the most expensive children's boutiques. She was proud, and I believe it brought her a sense of happiness when people would compliment us. She chose to have her daughters dressed up like royalty, but she neglected her own appearance. My mother's goal in life was to save enough money to build her dream house in Portugal. She also wanted us to pursue our education and graduate. Although my mother worked long hours, she did not have full control of her money. All her earnings were given to my father, and he controlled her finances. When it came to spending money on our clothes, she would lie to him and say that her employers gave her some hand-me-downs for the kids. When she needed to buy something for us, she would voluntarily work extra hours and ask to be paid in cash so my father would never know.

My mother was not allowed to buy anything without my father's permission or direction. When my father had opened his construction business, every bonus she received, and all of her savings had gone directly into his business. My mother had to sign every document he presented to her without reading or questioning it. My father always criticized her for not fully immersing herself in the Jehovah's Witnesses faith, but she refused to let go of her Catholic devotion. She was willing to open her door to the brothers and sisters, and even hosted many lunch and dinner parties with four-course meals for my father's guests. Occasionally, she would attend certain Jehovah's Witnesses events whenever Anais and I insisted that she join us, but otherwise she refused to embrace their faith.

My father would always instigate fights with my mother and wanted to stick it to her. He would hide behind the Bible to justify his rage. We always heard him calling my mother a "sinner," and her would spend weeks without speaking to her. My sister and I had to be the messenger back and forth because he would not say a word to her.

He would pick on the food she served and refused to eat it. My mother was an exceptional cook, yet he would pressure her to cook another dish and made her feel like she cooked something uneatable. He disregarded the fact that she suffered from depression and was exhausted from working long hours. They were both old-school, believing that it was the wife's duty to serve her husband. Every day, he would complain about something, and he was never pleased. Nothing was ever good enough for him.

Through work, my father met a wealthy older couple, Denise and Roger, who did not have any children. My father started doing free favours for them, fixing things here and there in their beautiful luxurious home. Of course, he did these favours with the expectation that they would repay him in another form in the future. Even though they were considered worldly, my father never shared with them he was affiliated with the Jehovah's Witnesses. He started to live a double life.

When I was six years old, Denise and Roger hosted a Christmas dinner for family and friends. My father brought pastries, an expensive bottle of wine, and a Christmas flower arrangement. Denise and Roger loved Anais: she was quiet, older, reserved, and kept her thoughts and opinions to herself. Roger disliked me because I would talk and move around too much. Denise was more welcoming than Roger, but she wasn't too patient with little children. I always had too many questions, and I seemed to always have an unfavourable answer at the tip of my tongue.

"Émilie, what did you do this week at school?" Denise asked me during a moment of silence at the table.

"Well, we did dictations, and I got a ten out of ten. And then we read *Le Petit Prince*. And then we got to draw houses and colour rainbows. And then we went to the gym and played dodgeball. And when we went to recess, we played duck-duck-goose and—oh! We even went to the park to pick walnuts and—"

"What an insolent child," Roger interrupted me openly. "The dinner table is meant for adult discussions only. Émilie is not like Anais. She needs to know her place."

I stopped talking. My parents never listened to me or asked how my day went, so naturally I got excited when Denise asked me this question. Anais always kept quiet around my parents and would mainly speak to me. My father never wanted us to interrupt him while he was watching television, and my mother was never home or had no time to listen to us.

When Denise and Roger heard that my sister was not baptized in the Catholic Church, my father made a calculated move. They expressed how pleased they would be to become my sister's godparents. And just like that, my father had Anais baptized in the Catholic Church. Jehovah's Witnesses were not allowed to step foot in a Catholic Church, yet here my father was baptizing his eldest daughter there for the sake of his sick, ambitious goal to win Roger's favour.

"You call me a sinner because I'm not a Jehovah's Witness. Meanwhile, I'm not the one who had our daughter baptized in a Catholic Church even though you are a Jehovah's Witness! You are fake! You are a hypocrite!" my mother said to him.

"Maria, I am not a sinner. You don't understand what I'm doing. I had Anais baptized for *us*. Trust me, this will help our family. Roger's contacts will secure me work in the future. Jehovah knows what I am doing," my father replied.

Since Anais was their goddaughter, my father speculated that perhaps they would leave some inheritance money to her since they had no children of their own. After Anais's baptism, my father continued to attend the Jehovah's Witnesses meetings and living as though the baptism never happened. He would preach about the Bible from door to door once a week, but we still lived in fear at home.

When he went out to work or to preach door to door, we kept the television low to make sure we could hear when his keys were unlocking the door. As soon as we heard them, we turned the television off and pretended we were doing homework or dusting the living room. If he caught us with the television or stereo on, he would harshly punish us. Anything that we did or didn't do was an excuse for him to mistreat us and make us miserable. We never grew up with bicycles because he believed they were a luxury, that they would give us too much freedom. We were not allowed to play outside, go to the park, or take part in extracurricular activities. Any field trip for school was always a no. Any time I questioned him or went against him, he would slap me and then punish me.

I knew he was going to punish me or hit me, but I could not silence my voice. He needed to know that I knew he was dishonest. He needed to know that I had a voice. He needed to know that he could punish me all he wanted, but he could not silence me or kill the inner fire within me. Although I feared him, my biggest fear was to surrender myself to him. I refused to surrender to his torment and be silenced like my sister and my mother. I was a fighter, and I needed to keep fighting back. He was not going to kill my spirit.

# III

## THE BLACK LEATHER BRIEFCASE

My father was a complex man. He was so talented at putting on a show for others that no one understood who my father truly was behind closed doors. He was not the father nor husband that he made himself out to be. At the Jehovah's Witnesses meetings, he would speak kindly to us and pretend that he cared about us in front of others, but his behaviour wasn't real.

"Émilie, why don't you sit next to Papa before the ceremony starts?" my father would warmly say to me.

When the ceremonial hymns began, he would place his hand on top of my shoulder and slowly rock me back and forth to the rhythm of the music. But at home, he behaved as though he resented us. It's like he wanted to see us suffer. He loved to throw in our faces that we were privileged to have food, that we were privileged to sleep on a bed.

Anytime someone tried to do something nice for us, he would dismiss the gesture. Sometimes the brothers and sisters in our congregation would invite us to take part in outdoor activities, but his answer was always a firm no.

When *The Ten Commandments* played in an afternoon matinee show in theatres, Anais and I were invited to watch the film with the Jehovah's Witnesses Group of Youth. The Group of Youth was mostly Jehovah's Witnesses in their late teenage years. The people in the group were all fairly nice, but there was an obvious age gap between us since most of them were close to their twenties. We didn't connect much with the group, but they were always welcoming to us regardless of our age. We had thought we could go to the movies with the Group of Youth without any trouble, since this was a religious excursion related to the content of our congregation meetings. Anais and I were super excited to go to the movies, as I had never seen a film in a theatre before in my life.

"Antonio, my son and I are chaperoning with the young crew of the congregation, and we are taking them to the matinee of *The Ten Commandments*. Would you let Émilie and Anais come with us next Saturday afternoon?" Sister Feli asked politely.

"Thank you, Sister Feli, for always thinking of us. You are too kind. But Émilie and Anais have other things that they need to do. Giving them too much freedom would not be good for them. They have too much time on their hands during the week and will need to be helping their mother around the house this weekend," my father replied.

"That's fine, because the film will be around for a while. If they can't come this weekend, then it would be my pleasure to take your beautiful girls on another weekend when they would be free. Maybe Maria would also be able to join us as well!"

"No. They don't deserve to go. Too much pleasure is not good for them. They need to understand that life is not about pleasure. They need to earn the privilege to get certain things."

Eventually, the brothers and sisters stopped inviting us to take part in activities because they knew my father was stubborn. He knew that my sister and I were excited to go to the movies with them, but it was as though it brought my father satisfaction to see the joy wiped from our faces. I always asked myself, "*Why did Papa want to be a father?*"

Any time he dismissed our requests to take part in the community events, I replayed the conversations in my head. I couldn't understand what I was doing wrong. I couldn't help but take his words personally. I wasn't sure how to change his mind. I wasn't sure how to be better in his eyes. After he forbade us from accompanying the Group of

Youth to watch *The Ten Commandments*, I approached him in the living room while he was watching a television documentary.

"Papa, why are we always being punished even though we didn't do anything wrong to deserve it?" I asked him innocently, hoping for a sincere answer.

"Émilie, you are interrupting my program. You do not question me. You have to learn how privileged you are. Without me and what I give to you, you would be nothing. You need to learn discipline and learn to obey. It is God's law: obey your parents. You are a rebel, Émilie. You will have to learn obedience with me," he replied with an angry and annoyed tone.

"Papa, why are you always mad at me? Did you find me in the garbage bins? It seems that I can never do anything right."

"You and your rebellious ways. You are the Devil's child. You do not question me, am I clear?"

Was I? Was I a bad child? Was there something wrong with me? I started questioning myself. Maybe I *was* bad. Maybe it was the reason I was not lovable. I always needed to speak my mind. I was certainly not like my sister. She did not create waves, she did not rock the boat, she did not poke the bear; in fact, she never questioned anything. She just sat there and took it. Why couldn't I do that? How could she just accept his dismissive words? How could I not keep my mouth shut? My tongue always had to speak, had to question. I couldn't help that my mind raced with so many questions. I just couldn't understand. Was I under the influence of Satan? *Was I?*

In 1987, I was nine years old and an avid reader. I began my reading journey right before I turned six. I was eager to learn and read on my own. Agatha Christie was my company—I devoured her books. They transported me to a world outside of my sad life. My father was not keen on the idea of his children reading anything other than Jehovah's Witnesses tracts or the Bible.

Thankfully, the school library opened my mind to the endless world of literature. Any chance I had to visit the library, I would borrow one or two books at a time. I used to hide them under my bedsheets, with Jehovah's Witnesses brochures laid out on my comforter or pillow in case my father came into my bedroom. I wanted to give him the impression that I was reading only Jehovah's Witnesses literature. A copy of the Bible was kept on my night table for decoration. I had a small nightlight close to my bedside that helped me read under my sheets at night. Bedtime was the only opportunity I had to read my books in private, but I always had to stay alert if my father was still awake. If I heard footsteps approaching my bedroom door, I would stop reading and tuck the books between the headboard and the mattress. Otherwise, I would reach over to the Bible and quickly open it to a random passage.

Through reading, I slowly developed an affinity for Nelson Mandela and Mother Teresa. I read a lot about their work, and they became my idols. My father usually watched history channels and documentaries. I paid attention to a few of the documentaries about them and became enthralled with their unique gifts. But something about them confused me at the time. Those who were not a part of the Jehovah's Witnesses were considered worldly and under the influence of Satan. So how could Nelson Mandela be persecuted and survive in prison, and still carry a message about love and hope? How could he be talking about freedom of the mind when he was locked up in prison? How could this man be under Satan's influence and be corrupted when he was suffering the consequences of speaking his voice against oppression and racism?

And what about Mother Teresa? How did this woman, who lived humbly and dedicated her life to serving the marginalized and advocating for the poor, be under Satan's influence? She spoke the language of the Bible, she lived with compassion, and she showed love toward others. She put her life in service to others and lived with love in her heart in the middle of misery and poverty. She did not blame nor condemn God, but she kept the flame of her faith alive and held strong while carrying others. It all felt so confusing to me.

I started to suspect that perhaps I was misguided. When I thought about these questions about Nelson Mandela and Mother Teresa, I wanted to ask my father for answers, but I couldn't. I would be punished for even questioning the slightest thing about our Jehovah's Witness faith. I felt like I was imploding. I wanted to know the truth!

My father was a very good speaker. His words were so eloquent that the brothers and sisters in the congregation would give him their undivided attention for what he had to say. He would charm them with intelligible conversations about the Bible, or about our recent discussions from the pamphlets. He strictly practiced against having unnecessary interactions with the worldly. He wouldn't even interact with his older sister, who lived in the same city as us, and we had to limit our interactions with my aunt and my cousins as well. We minimized our interaction with the worldly. I grew up knowing very little of my own family.

November 9, 1987 was a day that I will never forget. It was the day I realized that on a deeper level I truly did not know my father. That day was the first time I grasped an understanding of intuition, of what a gut feeling is. Earlier in the year, my father had decided to sell his luxury car. It was customary for my father to buy a new car every year. Since we would drive to Portugal for family vacations every summer, my father did not like the idea of his luxury car accumulating mileage and depleting the car's value for every round trip to Portugal. But this time around, my father had been struggling for months to find a buyer.

To top it off, my father had some issues at work. He had a construction crew working for him, and the foreman in charge was not managing the crew well. My father found him to be sloppy, disorganized, and untrustworthy in his way of work. He found him cutting corners on several tasks and noticed that this foreman would either over-order material or have little material available when they needed to meet deadlines. My father hated his work performance, and he could see that this foreman and his crew were costing his company money and his reputation in the construction business with their performance.

After a few visits to the site and warnings, my father eventually fired the foreman and his construction crew. Hearing this, the foreman was very upset and could not accept these circumstances. He expected my father to pay him a severance package, but he was not entitled to receive more than what my father had already paid to him. He started calling my apartment every day and making threats. Once my mom answered the phone and the foreman threatened to bring my father's head on a platter. My poor mom was scared and concerned for my father. She thought the foreman meant his words literally, and that one day he was going to kill him.

The evening of November 9, my father announced that he had found a potential buyer for his luxury car and this buyer was coming to check it out and take the car for a spin. I remember being agitated. I started feeling my heart racing and my chest tighten, almost if someone was sitting on it. I did not want my father to go by himself. Something strange had taken me over—an inner strength, a voice, something *powerful* in me. I needed to go with him.

"Maman, I am going to go with Papa," I said to her.

"Well, you'll have to ask your father," she replied. I walked over to my father as he was putting on his coat.

"Papa, I'm going to go with you."

"No. It is already dark, and I don't need you to come with me," he said. I walked back over to my mother, but this time I was feeling despair in my chest.

"Maman, I need to go with Papa! With everything that is going on, he shouldn't go by himself. You know this is true," I begged.

"Well, it's not in my hands. If your Papa doesn't want you to go, then it's up to him. You'll have to ask your father."

"Papa, I did all of my chores. I have all my homework done. Just let me go with you! You have to let me go with you!" I insisted.

My parents looked at me and gave me a weird look. My hands were shaking, and I felt like my heart was going to explode. They saw that I was pushy and agitated before they looked at each other.

"Okay. If your maman says it's okay, then it's okay," my father said. My mother nodded.

My father grabbed his car keys, brought out his black leather briefcase, and was ready to go. I put my shoes and my jacket on, and together we made our way downstairs. The parking garage was about a two-minute walk from our apartment. When we arrived at the entrance of our building, I stepped out onto the sidewalk first, my father trailing behind me. As I made my way in between the parked cars along the street, I looked over to my left and saw a man leaning against the church gate at the end of our street. My heart tightened and my hands started to sweat as soon as I recognized that it was his old foreman.

As soon as he caught a glimpse of my father, he raced toward us while gripping tightly to a dagger. With very little time to react, I knew what I needed to do.

"*Run!*" I screamed.

I opened my arms and threw myself in front of him in an effort to stop him from attacking my father. Watching this all unfold, my mother yelled in despair from the balcony at the top of her lungs. He backed me in between two parked cars where there was nowhere left for me to run. He raised his arm with the dagger in his hand and stared down at me, his bulging eyes filled with hatred. I thought that he was going to launch the dagger at me. I thought that this was the end. Before I knew it, I was launched onto the hood of a car. My body was so shocked and overwhelmed by the blow to my back that I could barely speak. I couldn't move.

"*Stop now!*" my father shouted.

I turned my head to the voice of my father. I saw something from the corner of my eyes: *a gun*. My father was holding a pistol to the foreman at point-blank range. He'd had it concealed in his briefcase the whole time. Once he caught a glimpse of my father's weapon, the foreman backed up from me and ran away, throwing the dagger in some garbage bags on the side of the road.

I was in shock and my body gave up on me for a moment—I couldn't move. My legs were like cotton, my back hurt, and I was still trying to process what had just happened. I couldn't believe my father had a gun. My mother had made her way down and was hanging on to me, crying hysterically. She was grateful that I was alive. She was grateful that I was unharmed. I was stunned, I felt numb. My thoughts were racing.

What happened? What was this? I could have died. *He* could have died. My mother helped me down from the windshield. She held my hand tightly and together we went back inside of our building.

"Are you okay?" my father said in a low voice before going up the stairs. He spoke quietly because he was concerned the neighbours would hear.

My throat was tight, so I nodded my head as I held my mother's hand. My mother was cold and shaken. I was trying to stay calm, because at times my mother would faint. I couldn't afford to have her pass out right now; I needed her. My tears were dropping silently down my cheeks, and the three of us climbed upstairs in silence. My sister was anxiously waiting in the hallway outside our apartment door and hugged me as soon as we approached her. She too was shaking and crying.

We took off our jackets and shoes by the front and silently made our way to the living room. My father held my hand and made me sit beside him. For the first time ever, I saw a blink of humility in his eyes as he thanked me for saving his life.

"My dear daughter, you gave me enough time to run. If it wasn't for you, I would not have had the time to run and scare him off with my fake gun," he said to me gently. "You are my little superhero!"

He was still holding my hand, and with his other hand he gently caressed my head. I could feel the warmth from his touch. I craved that affection and love so much. I leaned over and placed my head against his chest for a moment just to be close to him. Tears again fell silently from my face. I wanted to capture this moment forever.

I wanted to feel this forever. This moment was the closest I've ever felt with him. But it was short-lived.

He was on a mission to prepare the family for his next lie. He needed to call the police, but we were not allowed to mention anything about his gun.

"That gun you saw is a fake," my father said.

"Please, Papa, just tell them the truth!" I cried. "It was self-defence. It's not like you shot anyone. And it's a fake gun, so just show it and they will know it's a toy!"

"Antonio, tell the truth, because you don't know if our neighbours or the people in the buildings across the street heard what happened. What if they saw the gun? Can you just please show me the toy gun?" my mother asked.

"No. You need to do exactly as I am telling you or we will have serious problems and it will all be your fault," my father refused as he raised his voice at us. "If you tell them the truth, this will stain my reputation and it will have disastrous consequences for my business."

This request was very difficult for me. I felt sad, deeply sad. And I felt nauseated at such a horrible request. This felt like I was playing a role in a horror movie. He was making himself seem like he was the victim—really? I was about to give up my life for him. A nine-year-old girl processing a near-death experience, putting her life on the line to save her own father, and *he* was the victim? He was blaming us once again that if anything went wrong, if anything went against his plan, it would all be entirely our fault.

*I almost died for you, Papa, don't you understand? I love you so much that I would have died for you without blinking. And you are worried about your reputation?* I thought, replaying the conversation in my head.

As planned, we went to the police station. My father gave his statement, but it had been modified and it deviated from the truth. When it was my turn to give the police my statement, a female officer asked me only a few questions while the male officer typed the report.

"Hello Émilie, can you please explain what happened?" The policewoman asked politely.

I shared my experience with the officer, but I left out the details about the briefcase and the gun. I felt small. It didn't help that I already had to be dishonest with them. I barely made eye contact with the officers because I felt ashamed. I didn't mention my father's gun. I told them that we heard the voices of a group of adults approaching the street, then the foreman threw out the dagger and fled the scene.

"You're a hero! You saved your father's life," the policewoman said to me as she peeled off a superhero sticker.

It bothered me deeply that we couldn't tell them the truth, but this for my father was natural. My heart felt like it was coming out of my mouth. All of this didn't sit well with me, yet somehow, I felt only numbness and a deep sadness. I lost faith and trust in my father. Everything he said, everything he did—all of it was contradictory. It was all empty air. I had no idea what to believe in anymore, I just knew I was heartbroken. My heart ached, my body ached. That moment we had together earlier in the living room . . . would that ever happen again?

We were living a perfect life on the outside, a façade that was meant only for others to see. But it was all fake. There was nothing harmonious or happy about our lives. My mother felt suicidal and my sister had a life only when he was not home. The rest of the time she would carry herself through the apartment with a lifeless expression and just take orders from him as they came to her. I wanted to believe that my father would change. Dear God, I wanted so much to have hope and believe in my father. But he acted like a venomous spider, and he was filled with deception and lies. We were living in a cocoon of misery and pretending that everything was perfect as he wrapped us in his web of lies, one after the other.

It was at nine years old when I figured out one of the most precious lessons in life: we have an inner compass, and a choice to make in our life. We have a place to take on this world. If we listen closely, this compass gives us a sense of direction. It's a voice that urges us to listen; we just need to allow it. I never liked when people were dishonest—the truth may not be easy to share but lies leave lasting scars. And for once, I didn't like myself for being dishonest that night. That night, I let myself down. I should have used my voice and told the police the truth. I was scared of being honest because I didn't want to be responsible for bringing harm to him or my family. And suddenly, I knew that I had just become his partner in crime by being an accomplice with my silence. So I confronted him.

"Papa, what you made me do tonight was wrong. Lying is against God's law. I felt ashamed not to tell them the full truth. You have a gun, and we should have told the police that. It is always better to tell the truth!"

"Émilie, shut your mouth. Who are you to question my authority? You mention the gun one more time and I will make sure that you will not be able to speak for a week."

His words once again echoed in my little heart. I was drowning in a pool of my deepest thoughts and wishful thinking. I wished for a father who loved me, who cared for me, who protected me. A father who would smile when he looked at his children, who would laugh with his family. A father who would play with me, teach me, guide me, support me, cheer me on, who would see me, accept me, and, above all, love me unconditionally. A father I could be proud of.

# THE FALLEN EMPIRE

For several years, my father was a well-established residential developer whose company owned two real estate offices. His company built and sold newly constructed residential homes in the Chambéry region. But slowly, my father started to lose his grasp on his construction empire.

In late 1989, we were living in a mysterious atmosphere at home. It first started with my father coming home early from work. Then he would come home for lunch at one p.m., saying that he wasn't feeling well. Then there were days when he would stay in bed all day and complain that he felt sick. He started to avoid going to work and furiously demanded to get blood tests, MRI scans, ultrasounds, biopsies, and other absurd tests from our family doctor to prove that there was something wrong with his health. Even after completing these tests, there was nothing concerning in his results. His main issues were hemorrhoids and back pain that he had developed at a young age from working heavy construction. Other than that, my father was relatively healthy. He even changed family physicians and asked to retake these tests, yet we couldn't understand why. Even the new doctor didn't find anything of concern.

Since my father was home a lot more, we were suffocating from his constant presence. He watched our every move meticulously. I would be washing the dishes after lunch and feel him eyeing me from behind, watching every motion that my hands made with each wash, how much soap I dispensed into the sponge. Anais was in panic mode all the time. My mom started to become agitated, losing her temper easily and feeling more emotional. With my father home a lot more, my mother would cry often and lose her temper.

"Oh God, help me. I already have one foot in the grave. It would be better to just have both of them in," my mother said many times.

She was chronically exhausted from managing a household and her work demands. My father's unrelenting criticism must have made her feel like going to her death was better than living. Her despair did not need words, it was felt and my little heart ached for her. She looked drained and the dark circles under her eyes deepened. She was suffering from insomnia, so she asked our family doctor for something to help her ease her nerves.

Rather than addressing the cause of my mother's depression, she was prescribed an antidepressant which became known as "mother's little helper" because it numbed feelings, allowing women to move through their day. Rather than helping my mother, it just masked her depression, deepening her despair. She had suicidal thoughts, but because of cultural conditioning, talking about her emotions or reaching out for help was not an option. Occasionally, she would faint and sometimes it would take a while for her to regain consciousness. As a small child, I lived in constant fear and anxiety of finding my mother dead on the floor. Her words haunted me and became an unbearable burden of responsibility. I was so scared when my mother had to be home alone for long periods. I felt a tightness on my little chest and kept asking God to look after her when I couldn't.

In the spring of 1990, my father announced that he was forced to declare bankruptcy. He had too many clients that owed him money. He was not able to pay some bills and had accumulated debt. When my mother found out she was devastated and her whole world collapsed. She had worked long hours for many hard years, pumping all her income into his business, and now it was closing down. She did not know the extent of the mess that my father had created.

A few days after he announced his news, my mother sought help from one of her former employers to understand how her husband went bankrupt. Madame Bourgeois, a lawyer whose house my mother cleaned for a long time, was a friend of ours who had trusted my mother over the years. I used to play with her son, Nicolas, who was also my age. When we were five years old, we used to play every Wednesday morning while my mother was cleaning her apartment.

Madame Bourgeois loved my mother but despised my father. My father preferred obedient women, but Madame Bourgeois was strong and empowered, with good judgement of character, and did not give in to his manipulation. She could detect his bullshit. My father had approached her on a few occasions to defend him on his cases. She would offer him legal advice, but she knew better than to take on his cases because she found several gaps in his accounting and his stories—she knew he was hiding information. She knew my mother was a hard worker, who poured her life into her family and her earnings into my father's business. She knew that my father did very little to protect his family. She also sensed that he was not good to us.

Madame Bourgeois followed up with my mother after she sought help and told her that she had received access to my father's legal file. Madame Bourgeois confirmed that many people owed money to my father. It was due to his lack of accounting in his business that forced him to declare bankruptcy. He owed a lot of money in taxes to the government. She determined that he had not filed taxes for his business in a very long time. His bookkeeping was all over the place, and nothing was properly recorded or written clearly.

When my father opened his construction business in France, he did not register his business as a *société anonyme*, a type of business structure equivalent to a corporation. The benefit of a business registered as a *société anonyme* is that it limits the owner's risk of losing personal assets should the business go under. But my father never separated his business from his personal name. Consequently, after her visit with Madame Bourgeois, my mother learned that she too would be responsible for paying off his debt and taxes to the government because both their names were registered under his construction business.

We were going to lose our two apartments: the one we lived in and the one my parents used as a rental property. My mother was going to lose all her assets. The most difficult part for my mother to hear was that my father had actually sought legal advice from Madame Bourgeois in the past about his business. She had advised him to register his business as a *société anonyme*, but he never did. She also advised him to place the apartment ownerships under his children's names. This legal advice was the best way to proceed, because he would still take a financial hit but he would not lose all his assets, since the apartments would have been under our name. Of course, my father, with tremendous pride, refused to listen to her advice. Rather than being grateful for her help, he argued with Madame Bourgeois and stormed out of her office. There was nothing we could do, but this mess could have been avoided.

The judicial officers served my mother the court documents indicating that the process had already started, warning that all our assets were about to be seized. My mother would cry so heavily at home that she became unrecognizable. She was heartbroken, and I thought she was going to have a stroke by the way that she was shaking. That day when my father came home from work, she furiously confronted him in the kitchen while I listened from the other room.

"Antonio, you are so specific in watching everyone's movements at work. How did you miss the accountant not doing her work over the last three years?" my mother shouted, throwing the court papers at him.

"Maria, I am a victim of the system. They want me under because I'm an immigrant," he replied deviously. He was trying to manipulate her so she would feel sorry for him.

"Stop that! It's your fault that we are going under. You didn't do any of the legal measures that you were supposed to do. You were so proud of yourself that you couldn't even take any feedback or legal advice that was given to you to protect us."

"It's not my fault, it's the accountant's. She didn't do what she was supposed to do. I was framed; I am the victim here. You can't even see where I'm coming from, Maria. You don't want to understand."

"What's going to happen now? What are we going to do, Antonio? We're going to lose everything, that's what's going to happen to us!"

"I have the solution, the *right* solution for us. I've been thinking about this for a while. We should run away to Portugal, leave everything behind. We will leave in the middle of the night so no one sees us and we can start a new life, just like you've wanted. A life in our country."

"I am not going to run away. I am not a criminal. I didn't do anything wrong." My mother shook her head.

I couldn't believe the solution he proposed during their conversation. After hearing my father's news, and at the simple thought of moving to Portugal, my sister started crying. I felt very angry. I was tired of the shit that my father put us through. All our family's suffering fell into the hands of my father. He chose not to help himself at everyone else's expense. And now we needed to make a sacrifice? Fuck no.

The following morning, my father had left to preach door to door with other members of the Jehovah's Witnesses. Anais and I were finishing our teas in the kitchen while my mother was putting away dishes after breakfast.

"Maman, I am not leaving to go to Portugal. I don't want to leave my school. I don't want to leave France! I belong here! I would rather kill myself than leave. Maman, I will kill myself, but I will not go," my sister exclaimed.

Was she serious? Hearing these words come out of my sister's mouth hurt me deeply and worried me. I could not stop thinking about the amount of pain my dad brought to our family. His actions were having a direct impact on my mother and sister, but he was insensitive and inconsiderate to how his actions affected us. My sister was eighteen years old, an adult in France, but she was a prisoner to a fear that paralyzed her. She thought that the only alternative to going to Portugal was to end her life. It made me sick to see her endure this cycle of fear and pain. With tears in her eyes, my mother reached out for my sister's hand.

"Don't worry, don't worry, my daughter. I will not make you leave," she whispered to her as she gently grabbed her hand.

My mother turned to look at me. I could see her face filled with tears once more, and in the middle of the kitchen the three of us cried. For a moment we just stood there, holding each other's hands, and cried. It was a painful moment, but a comforting one as well. None of us wanted to be displaced from home.

"Émilie, how do you feel about moving to Portugal?" my mother asked.

"Maman, you know I love visiting and going to Portugal, but only as a vacation. I don't want to live there," I replied.

Don't get me wrong, I loved Portugal. We had family and friends there, and I loved the ocean, but living there was not an option for me. My sister and I spoke Portuguese, but we never studied the language in depth. Personally, I felt happier in my own country.

My father's older brother John lived in Portugal, and I adored him. We would visit him every summer. My father and uncle were complete opposites. Uncle John was a little bit shorter than my father. He had thick white hair and a huge tummy that reminded me of Santa Claus. My uncle was an honest man who lived by his words. He did not tolerate lies or injustice. He was strong in his beliefs, and he always spoke his mind. He treated us like the light of his eyes, the daughters he never had. Every summer, he would bring us so much joy trying to make us happy and create beautiful memories with us. As usual, though, my father disagreed with the affection that he expressed toward us. If we went to the beach and my uncle offered to buy us an ice cream, my father would always step in and argue with him. Everything was always an argument with my father. They would bicker about the way my father treated us.

"Antonio, who are you raising? Are you an army general? They are not soldiers; they are your daughters. They need your love! If you don't want them, give them to me," he once said to my father.

"You are not a father, mind your own business," my father replied.

"I would not want to be a father like you, for sure. I feel sorry for my nieces. On my watch, I will not let you treat them this way."

In our previous summer visits, we would leave my uncle's house earlier than scheduled because my father could not handle his criticism about his parenting. My father enjoyed punishing us by cutting our visits short the moment he became fed up with his brother. Uncle John loved us very much, and we felt loved and safe when he was around.

When my father returned home that day from door-to-door preaching, he was in a good mood thinking that we were all on board to moving to Portugal. While my mother was cooking lunch, he came into the kitchen and started teasing my mother with a joke that was not funny.

"Antonio, the girls and I will not be leaving with you to Portugal," my mother said to him definitively. "Running away is not the solution. You know I did not do anything wrong, so I have nothing to fear. I am staying in this country." Hearing this, my father's face dropped, and his mood changed instantly. He tightened his lips and folded his brows.

"Maria, you do not have a choice. We must leave. There are many people very angry at me because I cannot pay them. You are putting us in danger. We will be in danger if we stay here. We must leave. You are not understanding—this is the only solution we have," my father replied seriously.

"As I said before, I did not do anything wrong. I always worked honestly, so I have nothing to worry about. I am not going to just run away. It will seem that I did something wrong when I didn't. The girls don't want to leave either. Anais is eighteen years old and in the middle of her studies. I'm not ruining her life. I will not move," my mother responded assertively with a firm look in her eyes.

My father knew my mother's weakness. She worried about what people thought about us and about her. My father had been the director of the Portuguese Club in Chambéry. Since he was fluent in French and Portuguese, my father helped Portuguese newcomers integrate to the city. My parents were seen as wealthy in the Portuguese community because they owned two apartments and had a business. My father was well aware of how much she cared about her reputation in the Portuguese community.

"Maria, we are going to lose everything. How humiliating will it be when the whole Portuguese community finds out about this? We will have to rent an apartment now. We won't be homeowners anymore. How will you feel about this when people see us on the street and start talking about us? They will make fun of us," my father said.

"I will continue walking on the street with my head held high, because I did nothing wrong," she replied.

"I would rather be sick with cancer than have to work under someone else's company," said my father.

It was at that moment we finally understood why my father argued with our family physician and opted to switch to a different doctor. We found out later that he had asked our family doctor to diagnose him with pancreatic cancer, but our doctor refused to participate in his sick game. He wanted to trick us into falling for his plan to leave for Portugal, claiming that he was very sick and wanted to spend the rest of his years back in his home country. But who lies to this extent to their family? When was he going to stop this painful madness? How could he keep hurting us with his lies? It was because of my father's excessive pride that he fell into a downward spiral.

# FRENCH EXIT

A few weeks had passed since refusing to move to Portugal, and our home had fallen into a deep, intense silence. My father stopped talking to my mother. He spent most of his time reading the Bible and ordering Anais and me around. He was miserable and always angry. We could barely breathe at home. We only had a short break from him when he left the house or when we went to school.

In June of 1990, my father proposed another brilliant offer. He had found work in Bourgeaux, a small town that served as a transport hub in the winter for a ski station about 100 kilometres from Chambéry. He was offered a job as a foreman for a residential development project. With his experience in the industry, his salary would be high. The new company he worked for had found us a luxurious three-bedroom apartment in the middle of the town. The building had a parking garage with a remote-monitoring high-security system. The apartment was open concept and spacious with an unforgettable view. The kitchen and living room featured beautiful bay windows that faced the majestic mountains. We had a glorious balcony with enough space for tables and chairs so we could eat outside comfortably. It was a beautiful apartment, but our hearts were aching at the thought of moving away. We did not want to go anywhere.

Before we left Chambéry, Anais was finishing her accounting studies at a technical school. She couldn't exactly leave midway through her schooling, so the option for my sister was to stay behind with one of the families in the Jehovah's Witness congregation. She would continue with her studies and visit us every weekend. Even though we were not thrilled about the idea of moving, after some consideration my mother and I eventually agreed to move with my father, while Anais stayed back in Chambéry.

We officially moved to Bourgeaux in August of 1990. The school I enrolled in had dormitories and a cafeteria that served three meals a day. My school was hiring someone to fill the role of a cafeteria counter attendant. Fortunately for my mother, the cafeteria employed her to fill this role and serve meals to students and campus residents.

As his first priority, my father took it upon himself to connect with the Jehovah's Witness congregation in that small town, and we too were expected to attend the meetings every week. School had started in September, and for the first time in my life I was separated from Anais. It was hard for me. I knew no one in town, I felt like an outsider, and, more importantly, I felt alone. Since I was little, I hated to be by myself. I couldn't stand it. I feared the silence.

Despite the gorgeous view of the majestic mountains in my apartment, being in an empty house was unbearable at times. It was a few weeks into the new term and school was already difficult for me. As the newest student at the school, I was faced with discrimination and unacceptance once again. My peers knew that my mother was the cafeteria lady. My mother's attempt to speak French was masked by her heavy Portuguese accent. She served meals to the most spoiled and entitled kids. Some students would make fun of her behind her back, and sometimes a group of girls would approach me and share mean comments about the way she talked.

"Hey, you, your mom can't even say *s'il vous plait* properly! She says "si yoplait"—that means yogurt!" one girl would say, while the crowd of girls behind her snickered and shouted with laughter. "There is no place for people like her who don't even know how to speak French here. Go back to where you came from."

"I was born in France, just like you. This *is* where I come from," I retorted.

Some students were not receptive to different cultures or backgrounds. Being the daughter of an immigrant worker, I had faced some bullying and racism through most of my childhood at the private elementary school that I attended in Chambéry. Many parents looked at my mother with disgust, and they instructed their children not to play with me.

As I grew into my early teenage years, discrimination was still familiar to me. I could tell that I was going through puberty because my hormones were going crazy, and I was super sensitive to what people would say. It was hard to hear mean comments from my peers, and it was adding to the heaviness of my misery. My experience at school started to ease when I tried out for long jump and track and field. All practices and tournaments were held during school hours. Thankfully, I did not have to ask permission from my father to participate because technically it was not an extracurricular activity. I was talented in these school sports. When some of the student athletes saw my abilities and saw that I was an asset to their team, I received less hostility and more respect.

Another year passed after our move, and my sister finally returned home to us. She had finished her schooling. I was happy to have her back with me. Her year living with that family had been fun—she even learned how to ride a bicycle. She felt free for the first time in her life because she hadn't had to live in fear of my father. Her return was a transition back to hell for her.

We continued to receive legal documents in the mail, and my father kept insisting his position of innocence. As usual, he complained that he was a victim of the system and he had done nothing wrong. Then he would throw it in our faces that it was our fault for staying in France, that we should have just moved to Portugal to avoid all this legal trouble. He was furious at us and decided to teach us what he called a "life lesson." Since my sister and I had ruined his plan to leave the country, we were spoiled and entitled in his eyes. He decided that my mother was no longer allowed to go grocery shopping. If she went against him, he would make sure to throw out everything that she would buy. From that point forward, we were only allowed to eat chicken, lentils, sole, and soup. For fruit, only apples and bananas were permitted. We were not allowed to have any other fruit, no other foods. No cookies, no treats, no desserts. Nothing was allowed.

It didn't help that my mother was always working weeknights. My father would be the only one who prepared dinner, and he made it a point to cook only these dishes. His food was bland. He deliberately stripped the food of its flavour for punishment. He cooked with no salt, no pepper, few spices, and very little oil. He made sure that the chicken was overcooked to the point of being dry.

Thank the Lord my mother worked at the school cafeteria. She started bringing home leftovers from work and hiding them under our beds when she came home. We would eat this food before my father's meals, and that way we only had to eat a small amount of his cooking. After months of eating the same bland food every day, we got to the point where we wanted to throw up. Limiting our food wasn't the only punishment he used against us. My father also resorted to trying to scare us.

One afternoon, while I was at school and Anais was home alone, my father returned home unexpectedly to intimidate her. At that time, my father wanted to turn us against my mother by unveiling secrets from her past. My mother was previously married and had a son. Unfortunately for my father, my sister and I had found that out years ago. We also knew that my father had a daughter from a previous wife. He had skeletons in his closet too. So really, he wasn't revealing anything new to us about my mother. In his head, he thought we were going to condemn my mother for her past sins, but we knew full well that both of them had a life prior to getting married to each other.

After surprising Anais unexpectedly, my turn shortly arrived. A couple of weeks later, I was eating lunch at home and my father came home unusually. I told myself to eat faster so I could wash my plate and return to school. He sat beside me while I hurried to finish eating. That's when he started to pour his poison.

"I want to tell you about the maman that you think you know, but you don't," he said as he watched me chew my food as fast as I could. I tried to avoid making eye contact with him. "Your maman is not a good person. And she is a liar. You don't know all her secrets. She's the one who makes me suffer—Émilie, look at me when I'm talking to you!"

"Don't waste your breath, Papa. There is nothing you can say that is going to change the way that I see Maman," I said to him.

"You . . . you Satan child. I wish I could throw you out of this window," he said. His eyes were filled with hatred. I was caught off guard. I swallowed back my tears, and with a robotic reaction I stood up from the table with my back facing the bay window in the kitchen.

"Do it, Papa. Throw me out of the window and just kill me, once and for all! You have been killing me little by little anyway. Stop my suffering. Just do it!" I said with my voice raised.

Furious, he stood up from the table as well, but stormed out of the kitchen and slammed the apartment door behind him. As serious as I was when I said those words, I was shaking, my heart was pounding, and my chest was short of breath. My legs and hands trembled with fear. My father had just threatened to kill me, and I had seen the hatred in his eyes. My dad did not love me.

"Am I that bad that my own father wants me dead? *Am I?*" I shouted in the quiet apartment, hearing my voice echo back inside my soul. I cried heavily for a moment. I went to the bathroom to wash my face and collect myself before going back to school. My heart was bleeding with pain. I cleaned up, tidied the kitchen, and went back to school. I made sure to control my emotions so no one would see I was wounded.

During these recent tensions, my father would sleep alone in the third bedroom. He had minimal contact with us and would barely speak. He spoke to us only if we were in front of the brothers and sisters of the Jehovah's Witness meetings. He still worked to maintain the appearance of the loving father and ideal family man.

A week after this confrontation between my father and me, the beginning of the end happened. My mother was previously diagnosed with carpal tunnel syndrome on both of her hands, but she had been deferring her surgery for a while because she couldn't afford to miss work. Her doctors strongly advised against deferring her surgery, as they warned that she would be putting her hands at risk and have a longer recovery time. On the day of her surgery, the surgeon advised her to take a minimum of three months off from work for her hands to recover. Her surgery went well, though she had bandages wrapped around her hands and complained that she was in a great deal of pain.

A few days after her surgery, she received a registered letter from the government stating that they were going to start garnishing a percentage of her earnings to pay for my father's debts. My mother was in shock. She was devastated and wanted to know the truth. Even after receiving this letter, she still did not know how much money he owed to the government.

When my father returned from work that evening, we were all anxiously waiting in the kitchen. My mother couldn't wait any longer, and she confronted him about the letter.

"Antonio, what is this? They are threatening to take a percentage of my pay. How much do you owe? What did you do?" my mother asked him.

She was leaning against the kitchen stove, while my sister was behind her close to the door that led to the hallway to our bedrooms. My father was against the kitchen counter, holding the letter. I was sitting between the kitchen and the living room. I had a full view of my father's backside and only a partial view of my mother, since he blocked my view of her. He silently read the letter.

"I am a victim of the system. People owe me money! They should go after the people who owe me money too!" my father exclaimed in a stubborn tone.

*Click.*

I turned my head, first looking at Anais and then my father. I shrugged off the sound and looked at my mother.

"Antonio, stop with your lies. Don't you see this letter is from the court? It is a decision that they've made, a sentence. What did you do? How much money do you owe?"

*Click.*

"Now they are coming after me because of you, Antonio! Stop lying to me. I deserve the truth," my mother cried heavily, raising her voice, and losing patience.

*Click.*

"Maria, I am a victim! I worked hard for so many years, and now the French government wants to take my money," my father replied, trying to justify the contents of the letter.

"*Stop!*"

*Click.*

"Once and for all, own up to your lies. What did you do, Antonio?"

*Click.*

My father was furious. He approached my mother with heavy hands and, with great force, hit my mother's bandaged hands, which swung against the hood fan—*bang!* My sister ran to my mother as she lost her balance to hold her.

In a split second, I saw the source of where the click was coming from: his pocketknife. He kept opening and closing his knife under the counter where none of us could see it. He left it on the counter right before he lunged at her. Blinded by the screeching pain that erupted from my mother, I picked up the pocketknife.

"Stay away! Leave Maman alone or I will stab you!" I said instinctively, pointing the knife directly at him. My mother turned to look at me. My father turned around and his eyes widened at what was in my hand.

When I looked at him, I realized that I was holding his pocketknife and had it pointed at him. I dropped it and ran to the house of a sister from the Jehovah's Witnesses. For the first time, I told her what had happened to my mother. She advised me to call an elder of the congregation and seek guidance.

About thirty minutes went by, and one elder came over. I explained to him what had just happened and what my father had done over the years, including the way he treated us and how we moved from Chambéry because he went bankrupt.

"You need to pray to Jehovah because you are being tempted by Satan," the elder humbly said to me in an annoyingly calm voice. I wanted to slap his face.

*Excuse me? We were living with Satan*, I thought, wanting to say this to the elder but realizing I would just be wasting my time. I had already written him off and deemed his opinion useless. I couldn't tell if he wasn't taking me seriously because I was only thirteen, or if it was because he didn't believe what I had to say about my father. I just nodded in silence.

When I came home, I found that my father had left. My sister and mother seemed calmer but worried.

"Maman, how are you feeling?" I asked her.

"My hands are still in pain," she said.

The greatest pain was the emotional scars from the lies and years of abuse from my father. My mother knew something was going to happen, and she was scared of what he was going to do to us next. What were the repercussions? Luckily for us, we only had to wait a few days to discover what was in store.

Months after eating my father's punishment meals, he eventually gave up on cooking. We were still not allowed to eat croissants or biscuits, but we were able to buy groceries again.

April 4, 1992 was a day that changed our lives forever. It was a Saturday, and my father was working. We had a full day to breathe until he would return home. Saturday was the day we would get groceries and go to the market. My mother did not drive, so it would take us a few hours to shop around. My mother could not carry anything because of her surgery, so Anais and I carried the heavy grocery bags.

We came home from grocery shopping and ate a late lunch. We started putting the groceries away and cleaning the house before my father returned home. The phone rang around five p.m., and as usual I picked it up since my mother and sister hated answering it.

"*Allo?*" I answered.

It was my father's boss asking where he was. He hadn't shown up to work that day. I was confused and explained that he had left for work in the morning. The boss explained that he had gone to my father's site to find no one had seen him.

Our first reaction was that we needed to call the hospital. Maybe he got into a car accident or something. I called the hospitals in the surrounding area, but no one by my father's name had been admitted. In a flash, my mother stood up and went to the third bedroom. When she opened the closet, she knew. He'd left. His closet was almost empty. His Bible and his black leather briefcase were gone. My mother searched for papers, but they were missing as well. My dad had left us.

I couldn't explain the mix of emotions. A part of me was relieved that he was gone, but at the same time a part of me felt sad, confused, and scared. He just left us behind without thinking twice. My mother was stunned; we knew she was scared. He had left at a time that was critical for my mother. She was not working because she had to recover from her surgery. She knew she could not pay the rent because it was too expensive. We had to give our one month's notice to leave the apartment. We could not sleep that night, as so much was going on in our heads we needed to process. While we were watching TV in the living room, the phone rang at one a.m. My mother went to the phone—she felt it was him. She put him on speaker.

"*Allo?*" my mom answered.

"I left to live my life. The life that I want. You can all live yours without me. Forget about me. You are on your own now." He hung up. Those were the last words we heard from him for a while.

Honestly, at times I had secretly envisioned what our life would look like without him. We had suffered years and years of physical and emotional abuse, but he was my father. He was toxic for us, but he was my father. He continuously hurt us, but he was my father. I was not expecting him to abandon his family like that. He had apparently made his choice.

We were going to survive this. We survived all those years of misery, and together the three of us were going to get through this.

My mother was anxious to go to the bank on Monday. My parents had a little amount of money that would help us to survive for the next couple of months. My mother had also been putting money aside for a while now. It was not a lot, but she did not want to be left completely dry.

Monday came, and my sister and mother went to the bank to withdraw some money. To her surprise, she found nothing was left. My father had gone to the bank on Friday to empty the bank account completely. Absolutely nothing was left for us. How could a father do this to his children? But how could I expect anything else from him?

# VI

## BIRDS IN PARADISE

The days after my father left, we were busy finding a new place to stay as we needed to evacuate the apartment before May 1. One of the sisters in the Jehovah's Witness congregation rented small and cheap apartments, and coincidentally, she had one available for us. My mother's coworkers were very supportive. They checked in on us, brought us fresh vegetables and groceries. The Jehovah's Witness members strongly encouraged us to go to the meetings, because they believed that it was an important time for us to pray. With all that had been going on, we really didn't have much time to attend the meetings. We had asked the young brothers of the congregation to help us move our heavy furniture from the old apartment into the new one. All the packed items and lighter furniture would be moved by Anais and me. We had no choice but to ask the congregation for some help. Setting us up with a new apartment and helping us move out was the most help we received from the congregation.

We didn't argue when they urged us to attend the meetings. The last thing we needed was an annoying lecture from one of the elders. We also had to sell some of our belongings because we didn't have the space to fit everything in our new apartment. We ended up storing the belongings we couldn't sell in the cellar of the new apartment.

Even though my mother was not cleared to return to work, she had already started calling people in Chambéry to look for work and a temporary place to stay. She knew she would have to start working to get back on her feet. With summer approaching, many

Portuguese people would be going on vacation, so replacements in the housekeeping and cleaning industry were needed. We were planning to return to my hometown.

By June, my mother had already started working a few days in Chambéry. She was temporarily living with a single Portuguese lady that lived in a one-bedroom apartment. Although my mother slept on the floor, she was grateful she had found work and a place to stay. The so-called worldly people were the ones who helped my mom find a new place and work, not the brothers and sisters of the Jehovah's Witness congregation. They offered us unsolicited advice on how we needed to manage our time to attend the meetings. We felt unsupported by them, and Anais and I felt disconnected from the congregation.

As Anais was looking for work in the accounting industry, she was working full time cleaning offices early in the morning, and in the evenings both my mother and my sister were cleaning bank offices together. Anais was also studying for her driver's license exam, so her time was limited. With all the living expenses and bills to pay, my mother was working day and night at the expense of her health. She started to feel pain in her joints, and we were worried about her. She had a week where she couldn't move her body. Her ankles, her knees, her elbows, and her shoulders felt like they were attacking her; it was as if her body was shutting down.

By June of 1993, I had completed my school year and passed my final exams. My grades were exceptionally high, and I was talented in French. Throughout my early childhood I had dreamed of becoming a teacher. I truly saw myself as an elementary instructor. My peers and even Anais would come to me and ask if I could proofread their French work. My teachers had always enjoyed reading my essays, and they would comment on how eloquent I was in expressing myself. For instance, I loved writing poetry. I found healing in writing, as I could express my deepest feelings. I knew that my mother did not have money to put me through university, between the costs of dormitory living, school tuition, and books. To the unpleasant surprise of my French teacher, I applied to a hairstyling apprenticeship because I knew that route would be the quickest way to earn money to help my family. The apprenticeship program was set up in a way where I would be working for three weeks straight, and I would be attending school for a week. I needed to help my mother with the expenses, so making money from the apprenticeship program was the decision I felt I needed to make to support my mother.

My mother's health continued to decline. She had days where she could barely walk or get dressed, yet she would still find in her the energy to work despite her pain. She was also worried that if she missed work, she would not be able to pay the bills. She was under a lot of stress, being the sole provider. In a few months, she went to various medical centres to complete assessments and tests. After all the testing, she was diagnosed with rheumatoid polyarthritis, which is an inflammatory and autoimmune disorder. My mother was experiencing pain that affected more than four of her joints at the same time. Her work only aggravated her symptoms, and it placed a lot of stress on her wrists and hands. She was still facing challenges with my father's unresolved bankruptcy from his construction business. She was receiving letters from the government, lawyers, and suppliers demanding the money owed to them. My mother had travelled to Portugal for a week in hopes of withdrawing some money from one of the joint bank accounts that she shared with my father.

To her surprise, she found nothing was left in Portugal. Her bank accounts were empty. My father, who knew the directors of a few banks in Portugal, managed to forge my mother's signature and withdraw all her funds without her knowing. When my mother told Madame Bourgeois about finding her bank account completely empty, Madame Bourgeois wanted to start a legal procedure in Portugal against my father. However, we had no idea where my father was, and my mother did not have money to hire a lawyer.

My mother declined proceeding with legal action against my father in Portugal because she couldn't afford it. The only thing she wanted and worked on with Madame Bourgeois was to be clear of any responsibility to pay for my father's business debts—that's all she asked for.

In the summer of 1993, Anais and I finally decided to disassociate ourselves from the Jehovah's Witnesses. After my father left us, it was clear to us that the brothers and sisters were only interested in our attendance in the weekly meetings and our preaching hours. They hadn't been understanding that Anais and I needed to prioritize our time to help our mother. We felt that they were always judging us on how we spent our time, and we were not happy there. We no longer wanted to continue pretending that we belonged to this faith. We each wrote a letter to the elders of the Jehovah's Witnesses and informed them that we were resigning from the faith. We were looking forward to the new life ahead of us.

In our letters, we explained that our values and beliefs were no longer in keeping with the Jehovah's Witness faith and going forward we would be voluntarily removing ourselves. We knew that as soon as we removed ourselves, members of the Jehovah's Witnesses were no longer allowed to speak with us because we would become unworthy.

Once the congregation received our letters, an elder from the congregation came to our apartment to condemn us for putting our time and material needs before Jehovah.

"If you trust Jehovah, and you come to the congregations as you are supposed to, then Jehovah will always provide for you and protect you," the elder said, showing us a passage from the Bible that he brought with him.

"Okay, so we are both going to stop working at night and go to the meetings. By the end of the month, will Jehovah give us the money we need to pay our bills?" I asked him sarcastically.

"Look at those candlesticks on your table." The elder pointed to the sterling silver candlesticks on one of our decorative tables. "Are you working for luxury? Are those essential to your lives? You need to put Jehovah first."

"Those candlesticks belong to my mother. Thankfully, my father didn't steal those from her when he stormed out of our lives and left us with all his debts. You're in our house, and our decision is made. You are the confirmation that we are doing the right thing. I think it's time for you to go," I said to him, gesturing with my arm to the front door. We felt at peace with our decision and free to move on with our lives.

My parents had Portuguese family friends known as the Sevilha family who they had known for several years, long before I was born. Valerio Sevilha, a close family friend, worked with my father in France. Valerio was a well-built construction worker with a classic buzz cut and gentle eyes. Valerio's wife Tina had short curly hair, was fit like Valerio, and loved to wear black. Valerio and Tina were like my aunt and uncle. Before my father converted to the Jehovah's Witnesses, my parents had baptized one of their sons.

My mother had reconnected with many people after my father left, including Tina and Valerio's family. They had asked my mother if she would allow me to go to Portugal for the month of August, since I was the only one who was not working that month. My apprenticeship was starting in September, so the timing was perfect. They had space in their car, so my mother felt it would be a good idea for me to travel and visit family friends.

After about twenty-four hours in the car, we finally arrived in Portugal, it felt surreal. The last time I visited Portugal, I was eleven years old, and it was our last family vacation. Four years had passed, and I felt more grown up than I was on my last visit. Tina and Valerio lived in France, but they also had a home in Portugal on a land that my father originally owned. The days following my arrival were accompanied by several family visits. Relatives from Tina and Valerio's family were very happy to see me. It had been four years, and they made me feel so appreciated and welcomed. It was a pleasure to see everyone, and it felt nice to feel this sense of love from the family. Being with Valerio and Tina gave me so much freedom to visit the beach or go to town whenever I wanted with their kids. I was so used to feeling like a prisoner whenever I visited Portugal with my own family that it felt liberating to be with Tina and Valerio, since they were so laid back.

During the summer in Portugal, small towns would celebrate *festas de Verão*, which were the traditional yearly summer festivals. Each town had a saint they honoured, and every day the different towns arranged live bands to perform in front of a church or in the town square. By Sunday, a liturgical proceeding would take place in the small town to honour the saint. When Tina's small town, Cama da Vaca, started to celebrate, they had live music and dancing every night for six days.

Every summer, Tina's sister Laureana and their brother Caetano would get together on a family vacation to celebrate the summer festivals. All three had kids around my age, and I always got along with them. The first night of the summer festival, we danced and partied until three a.m. We arrived at Laureana's house and decided to sleep on the floor. Caetano's son Pedro arrived that morning and woke us up by throwing water on all of us who were sleeping on the floor.

It was already late when we were woken up. Tina's son Miguel, Pedro, and I went back to Tina's house to shower and get ready for another night to party in town. By the time we got to Tina's house, Tina and Valerio had already left. The boys gave me priority to shower first. While I was drying my hair, Miguel walked toward me holding two men's shirts.

"What are these for?" I asked. He smiled, held me by my shoulders, and kissed my head.

"Who is the best cousin in the world? Who is going to iron my shirt and Pedro's shirt? Did I tell you how much I love you, cousin?" Miguel said to me with excitement.

"Smart ass," I said and rolled my eyes. We were like cousins indeed. After my father left, we were allowed to associate with the so-called worldly types again, so our families became very close. This smart ass knew how to trick me into doing things.

While I was ironing their shirts, Pedro came beside me shirtless to pick up his freshly ironed shirt.

"Thank you for ironing my shirt. I appreciate it," Pedro said to me.

I felt embarrassed when he walked in shirtless. Pedro was charming, with the most beautiful green eyes. His muscles were well defined, and his cologne was intoxicating. I did not want to stop smelling his cologne. As soon as I gave him his shirt, I snapped out of whatever was happening to me.

The three of us were finally ready to make our way to the party, which was about a twenty-minute walk from Tina's house. A car approached us on the road and got too close to me, but Pedro grabbed me by the waist and pulled me close to him.

"Thank you," I said shyly.

I started to walk a little faster. I felt my heart racing but could not understand why. When we arrived at the town square, we parted ways. Laureana invited me to dance, and we were laughing because I was telling her that she needed to be careful not to step on my white sneakers.

From out of nowhere, Pedro swept me away from her and we started dancing. His cologne was intoxicating. His hand was on the lower part of my waist, and he held me close to him. Our bodies were synchronized to the rhythm of the music, and I could feel my body surrendering to his hands. I needed to take control and not show emotion. At the end of the song, I smiled and thanked him for dancing with me. Tina was going to leave the party; she was tired and did not want to stay another late night. Knowing this, I made sure to jump on the opportunity to leave with her as fast I could. I went home with them while the younger crowd stayed behind.

The following day, Tina and I went to the beach together. It was nice to have a little quiet time. We were always surrounded by a lot of people, so it was pleasant to just relax and catch up with each other. When we returned to Tina's house, everybody was there. Caetano's sister-in-law was getting married in Lisbon, and as the adults were chatting, they proposed that the younger crew should go to Lisbon earlier than the adults to help the bride's family prepare for the wedding celebration.

The younger crew agreed, and we packed our bags that evening to leave for Lisbon the following morning. I had very few memories of Lisbon. There is so much history in the beautiful city, and the streets are arranged in many mosaic patterns. I felt connected to Lisbon's energy, architecture and detailed pathways.

Caetano's family lived in a three-bedroom apartment on the ground floor of a building. I could jump out of the window to access the street, that's how low the windows were to the ground. There was a community club on their street where locals in the neighbourhood would gather and socialize. The lifestyle in Portugal was different from what I was used to, and Caetano's family seemed to party all the time.

I finally met Sara, the bride-to-be, and she was lovely. She was going to have her bachelorette party that night. There were over twenty women participating in the festivities. We visited many bars and clubs where there was live music and dancing. That night, I lost control of my body for the first time in my life. Sara served me a caipirinha, a Brazilian cocktail that was sweet but heavily concentrated with cachaça, a Brazilian rum. By the end of the drink, I was a little tipsy and had a second glass lined up for me. I only had a few sips, but I was all dizzy. I couldn't stop laughing and my body felt free and relaxed for the first time.

We went clubbing and I danced my heart away. By the time we went back to Caetano's street it was around 3:45 a.m., and I ordered an espresso with a bit of lemon to help me clear the fogginess in my head. The night of Sara's bachelorette party, the groom was celebrating his bachelor party. All the guys from the party were standing outside, waiting for the bride to return. I sat on the first step of the building, waiting for someone to open the door so I could go back to Caetano's apartment. I felt a little weak, and I was ready to go to sleep. Pedro walked toward me and enchanted me with his charming smile.

"How are you feeling?" he asked me flirtatiously, knowing that getting tipsy was a new experience for me.

"I'm good. I just want to go to sleep," I said.

Jesus, we just got here, and he already suspected that I was a little drunk. The news travelled fast. I stood up because someone was approaching the stairs to get inside the building, so I leaned against the side. Pedro stepped closer to me and looked at me with his penetrating eyes, softly caressing my cheek.

"I am glad you are okay, and you chose not to drink more. I know how my family is, and they like to push people to drink and do stupid things. I know you are different. I'm happy to see you are okay, beautiful."

There was a pause. I could not say anything. How could I answer that?

"Would you be able to open the door? I really want to go to sleep," I asked him politely. He opened the door, and everybody went inside to go to sleep.

The following day, the house was in pure silence after the late night. Everybody was still asleep. Being an early bird, I had peacefully showered. When I was about to sit to eat my breakfast, Sara, the bride-to-be, knocked on the window of Caetano's apartment.

"I would like you to come help me choose some flowers for my wedding this afternoon. Would you? Oh, and Pedro and Miguel will be coming with us," said Sara enthusiastically.

"Sure, I'd love to!" I said, feeling honoured that she chose me to give my opinion on her wedding flowers.

We had lunch at Caetano's apartment, and then we took the subway downtown. When we came up from the subway, we walked toward the flower market and I could feel the unforgiving heat giving me a sunburn. The flower market was beautiful. I was surrounded by a diversity of tropical flowers with beautiful colours. Every time I looked up from the birds of paradise, a flower from the Portuguese island of Madeira, Pedro was staring at me with a shinning smile.

While we strolled together side by side, he asked me questions about my life: if I had a boyfriend, what my career goals were, my dreams and aspirations. He also asked some questions about my father, whom he had met when he was younger. I reciprocated the conversation and asked him about himself. He was twenty-two years old, he worked at one of the health care centres in Lisbon as a caregiver for three years, and he was expecting to grow in his career. He made sure to tell me that he was single, and that his last relationship was a long one with a co-worker who was a single mom.

He knew I was a fifteen-year-old who'd never had a boyfriend. He kept smiling at me and looking at me with his dazzling green eyes. I noticed that he smoked a lot—he seemed to always have a cigarette in his hand, and I did not like that.

After a few hours at the flower market, Sara finally picked out the white lilies and roses she was looking for. On our way home, Pedro sat beside me on the streetcar and the subway. His leg was touching mine, and even if I tried to pull away, he would find a way to feel my leg again. When I gave him a sharp look to signal that I was uncomfortable, he would gesture back with a flirtatious smile.

When we got back to Pedro's apartment, everyone had already left to go to the community club. Pedro was pleased. He grabbed my arm and turned me around slowly.

"Why don't we stay behind and continue our conversation?" he asked me.

My head told me to go to the club, but my mouth replied yes. We sat close to one another at the table, his legs touching mine. He had served me a glass of ice water after the hot day at the market. I was nervously playing with my glass when he grabbed my hand and started kissing it. My heart was racing so fast I thought it was going to explode. I felt butterflies in my stomach. My whole body was awakened by his touch.

"I think we should join the others at the club. Let's check if Aunt Tina and your father have arrived yet," I said to him. Caetano and Tina were waiting for us at the club and dinner was served when we arrived.

After dinner, and to prepare for the following day, I went back to Caetano's apartment to iron my dress and get my heels ready. I was planning to wake up early to get my hair done with the bride at the hair salon. I always preferred to organize myself, but I was confused how Pedro's entire family, including his mother, didn't seem too concerned with preparing themselves for the wedding. Pedro was the best man, yet his dress shirt and his pants weren't even ironed. From behind me, Pedro was smiling and observing every move I made as I ironed my dress.

"I can't stop looking at you, Émilie. You are so beautiful. You mesmerize me. I just want you to kiss you," he said.

I shook at the sound of his voice. For a moment I got scared because I was caught off guard that he was watching me from behind. He walked toward me and swept me from the floor with one hand around my waist. He pushed me toward him and passionately kissed me. His lips were sensual, soft, and warm. My body felt a rush of energy, and I surrendered to him. I felt like I was in a movie scene.

When I heard someone walking toward the living room, I pushed him off me. His eyes were still filled with passion. His sister opened the apartment door, and I pretended that I was putting my dress on the hanger. She did not seem to understand anything. My head was racing with so many thoughts: what just happened? What did I do? If my mom knew, what would she say? What was Tina going to say if she found out? Was Pedro playing me?

I couldn't stop thinking about my mother as well. What would she think if she found out? I even thought about Jehovah too. I was raised in a religion that condemned any intimacy before marriage. And even though I was no longer a Jehovah's Witness, I was feeling guilty for having kissed Pedro. It almost felt as though I had committed a sin. I knew that the right thing to do at this moment was to head straight to bed.

On the morning of the wedding, everyone was still sleeping when I got up. I showered and woke up the bride for our hair appointment. I still couldn't stop thinking about what happened the night before, and it didn't help that Sara mentioned on our way to the salon that Pedro was fascinated by me.

When we returned from the salon, the apartment was pure chaos. People were shouting to hurry up to take their showers; people were rushing back and forth between rooms trying to find something; clothes were all over the living room waiting to be ironed; bedrooms had makeup spilled all over the floor. While everyone was going crazy, I felt at ease knowing that my hair was done and my dress was already ironed.

Pedro wore black pants, a white dress shirt, and a beautiful salmon tie. I could smell his cologne from the hallway. He turned to me and kissed me in front of his cousins without any concern.

"You look so beautiful, Émilie. I missed you. I couldn't wait to see you today," he said.

I was embarrassed, but I kissed him back. I excused myself and went to the bathroom to put on my dress. The hairdresser had applied a light amount of makeup to my face, and I indeed looked beautiful that day. I wore a light green satin dress and it fit me perfectly. Everyone complimented my dress, including Caetano, Pedro's mother, and Tina.

When we arrived at the entrance of city hall, Pedro was taking advantage of the photographer taking pictures of the bride in front of the entrance. He walked toward me with his sparkly smile and gave me a kiss. While the ceremony took place, I made sure to stay as far away from him as possible because I did not want to draw any attention to myself.

I started to sense that Tina and Caetano were observing my interactions with Pedro. I felt that I was doing something wrong, and I needed to stop . . . but how could something feel so wrong and so right at the same time? The reception was a success. Pedro was supposed to sit at the bride and groom's table since he was the best man, but he chose to sit next to me at my table instead.

Pedro professed his love to me when we were alone at the table. "I have never met anyone like you before. You are sweet, gorgeous, elegant, and smart. You are everything that I look for in a girl, Émilie. What we have is love at first sight, and I think I am falling in love with you."

He looked at me and held my hand. He gave me one more kiss before he stood up to call his father and Tina over to our table. Tina had been watching us from afar, and I could tell that she was a bit stunned when Pedro and I kissed. Like me, the only thing Tina thought about at that moment was my mother. Pedro told them that he fell in love with me and wanted to spend more time with me. Caetano seemed concerned, and he reminded him that I was a family friend of theirs, that I was only fifteen, and that he needed to express his intentions with me clearly. I was supposed to leave Lisbon and head back to Tina's town after the wedding, but Pedro eventually convinced Caetano and Tina to let me stay in Lisbon a little bit longer.

In our time together in Lisbon, Pedro and I went on a few dinner dates, and right before I left for France, he offered me a promise ring. He bought one for himself and one for me. The ring resembled a gold wedding band but was much thinner. The ring was symbolic that we were committed to each other. I had fallen in love. I came back from a summer in paradise where everything felt magical, but my joy soon came to an end.

During the drive back to France, I kept thinking about my mother's reaction. My mother and Anais were to pick me up from

Tina and Valerio's apartment. When my family came, I gave them a big hug as soon as I saw them. My stomach was in knot—I was worried about breaking the news to my mother.

Tina offered my mother a coffee, and we sat around the table. She broke the news to my mother. Tina explained that I was interested in her twenty-two-year-old nephew. My mother knew who he was, but she only remembered him as a child. She was not happy at all; I could sense it. Tina reassured my mother that Pedro had good intentions and was working to grow in his career. However, my mother reminded me that I was too young to be in love, and I had more important priorities. I needed to think about my school and my future. She strongly believed that long-distance relationships never worked.

On our way home, no one spoke in the car. My mother was disappointed, and she was not ready to listen to anything I wanted to say. The next day was a Sunday, and during breakfast I tried testing the waters with her, but she lost her temper.

"If I knew you were going to be acting this way, I would have never let you go to Portugal. I am so ashamed of your actions, and you should be ashamed of what you did. Did you do anything with him?" she questioned.

"Of course not. How could you even think your daughter would lose her virginity like this? You can take me to the doctor if you don't believe me," I replied.

I was disappointed to hear her comments. I didn't do anything more than kiss Pedro, yet she was doubting me. For the first time, she made me feel how my father used to make me feel about myself. It's like my mother forgot who I was.

# VII

## THE DISTURBING RED FLAGS

September started, and so did my apprenticeship at a hair salon. My employer was old-school, so even if the salon was empty, we were not allowed to sit down all day. I would work eight long hours at the salon, and in the evening after work I would help my mother and Anais clean the bank offices to help pay for the bills. My mother was still dealing with the courts to clear herself of my father's debts.

At the same time, we were receiving phone calls and letters containing threatening messages. We thought it was the foreman looking up my family name in the city's phone directory. Sometimes we thought my father was sending threatening letters to play tricks on us. It got to the point where I was so scared that I would keep a knife inside my sleeve at night when we came late from work, holding the tip of the knife in my hand in case I needed to defend my family. I was only fifteen, yet I had to work all these hours, attend legal proceedings with my mother, and be always on guard. I was always in a fight-or-flight response, and it was an intense amount of pressure. I was so sick of it. What other teenager had to deal with this shit?

Ever since I returned from Portugal, my relationship with my mother felt strained. I could sense that she was disappointed in me. Every letter and phone call from Pedro made her upset with me. Having a civilized conversation with my mother was almost impossible. Any conversation we had resulted in the same argument: all men were the same, she was robbed by my father, she was sacrificing herself to give a life for me, she had been abandoned by my father and left with nothing after all her years of hard work. I tried to convince her to look past my father for leaving us, but that would just aggravate the situation. She accused me of not caring and for being insensitive to her suffering. It was exhausting.

At times, I wished she could see that we all shared the same pain as her. But her emotional distress blinded her. Her despair blinded her. It was difficult for me to see her disapproval every time she looked at me. I knew that my mom was disappointed in me, and I felt that even though I was trying my best to please everyone, I was constantly failing.

It started getting to the point where she would avoid making eye contact with me. In the past, she had always been harder on me than she was with Anais. I never really understood why. I guess it was because I was outspoken and always had an answer at the tip of my tongue. Now I felt that part of it had to do with the fact that I had a boyfriend. The more upset she was with me, the more disconnected I felt from her. That's when I started to feel closer to Pedro. I longed for nothing more than to escape my life in France and join him in Portugal. He was my ticket out of hell.

During the winter of 1993, Pedro mailed me a few gifts and one of them was a proposal ring. Pedro formally called my mother and asked her for my hand in marriage over the phone. My mother mentioned that we would be going to Portugal next summer. Her condition was that if Pedro and I were still together by the end of the summer, she would give him her blessings.

When summer of 1994 came around, we visited Pedro's family in Portugal. Pedro surprised me with his purchase of a two-bedroom apartment in preparation for our wedding. Seeing how committed he was, my mother finally agreed to sign the emancipation papers to allow me to get married to Pedro the following year. When we returned to France, we had to deal with ending my apprenticeship and processing my dual citizenship papers. When all was organized for me to leave, we bought my wedding dress at a boutique.

By the time November hit, I was finally prepared to move to Portugal to live with Pedro's family. My mother and I returned to

Portugal together that month, and she stayed with me for a few days to help me transition. My heart felt sad and conflicted; I did not want to be away from my mother. I knew she and my sister would miss me, but I couldn't handle living at home anymore. I felt like I was suffocating with all the pressure that was put on me.

As soon as I moved to Lisbon with Pedro's family, I managed to find work as an apprentice in a high-end hair salon that served many theatre and movie actresses. I was excited about that. Thankfully, the salon was about a five-minute walk from Pedro's parents' apartment and his work. Everything seemed to be falling into place. Pedro's father, Caetano, was a kind, hilarious, and genuine man. We had espresso in the morning together, and we exchanged stories about our families. I could tell he was a true family man, and I longed to have a father like him. In a way, I was grateful for marrying Pedro because I truly loved his father. It was like I was given a father as well.

Pedro's mother, Paula, on the other hand, was initially warm but soon became a nightmare. She was shorter than Caetano, a little plump, and had long grey hair. She was nosy and brutishly inserted herself into anything and everything happening at home or outside. She did not work and would spend most of her mornings in bed. She would get up and start her day close to noon. The rest of her day would be spent at a coffee shop, dining out and gossiping with some of her neighbours. Having been raised by a mother who was a cleaning lady, I was not used to Pedro's messy apartment. Dirty dishes would be left in the sink, countertops would be dusty, unfolded clothes piled up in laundry baskets left outside of the living room, shoe-print tracks were scattered throughout the whole apartment, and dust bunnies were living under every piece of furniture. The first time I ever saw a cockroach was in the hallway leading to the bedrooms.

It was obvious that for people who had plenty of free time on their hands, Paula and the rest of Pedro's family neglected to take care of their apartment. Living there was a very different lifestyle for me because I grew up in an apartment that was spotless. I was also raised not to gossip, and to mind my own business. Because my mother worked long hours all the time, she had absolutely no time or the will to gossip. Back in my hometown, some Portuguese ladies would share some of the latest news about the Portuguese community with my mother. Most of the time, my mother already knew about the gossip they shared, but she would pretend not to know and wouldn't contribute to the conversations either. She always tried to be neutral and would not speak about the lives of others. She raised Anais and me to not fall into the traps of gossip.

On an afternoon I was off work, I was cleaning my bedroom and doing my laundry. It was nice to have my own space; my bedroom was the only room in the house that was spotless and neat.

As I put away some laundry in the closet, I noticed that a few things were missing in my bedroom. First it started with my jewellery. I had placed a necklace and the matching bracelet at the corner of my vanity mirror in a white and grey box. I wouldn't touch them unless I went out on special occasions, so I knew exactly where I left them. But then I noticed that a few of my clothes were missing. When I went searching for my beige cardigan, I noticed it was missing from my closet and the laundry basket. I knew exactly how my clothes were organized, so it was strange that they had started to disappear.

"Paula, did you by chance see my beige cardigan? I remember washing it and air drying it on the balcony, but it's not outside anymore," I asked.

"No. I don't even know which one you are talking about. I don't think I've seen it," she replied with a dismissive tone.

I always disliked when people touched my clothes without asking. Heck, I wouldn't even allow my mother or Anais to touch my things without asking me first. I knew that something was not right, so one day I decided to take my lunch break an hour earlier than usual when I knew no one would be home. I went inside Paula's bedroom, and as I suspected, my necklace and bracelet were on her vanity. I wondered if Pedro's sister Simona had any possessions of mine. Feeling curious, I went inside Simona's bedroom and found that two of my shirts and my missing cardigan were in her bedroom the whole time. I felt betrayed. My privacy was invaded, and it didn't help that Paula lied to me too. Now that I had confirmed that they'd been taking my belongings without asking, I remembered that I had left twenty euros inside the back pocket of a pair of my jeans. I hadn't worn them in a few weeks, so when I went to check my jeans inside my drawer, the twenty euros were gone. I was absolutely certain I had left a twenty-euro note in the back pocket. It should have been there; I hadn't spend money on anything recently. I left the apartment and returned to the hair salon fuming.

My first client of the afternoon was an acquaintance of Pedro's family. For most of her life, she had lived on the same street as Pedro's parents. She knew I was his fiancée and had requested to have me apply her hair colour. I was still livid from my discovery earlier, but I had to maintain my composure in front of customers until the end of the day. I finished applying the dye to her hair, and before I left her for the waiting period, she reached out and grabbed my hand.

"Listen, Émilie," she said in a serious tone, "I need to warn you. You are such a special young lady. You are beautiful and very bright, but you are also very young. I am not sure you know the family you are entering. Pedro is a good guy, but he is also Paula's son. She is fake, manipulative, and dishonest. She lies and she steals. She is spiteful and her lies are dangerous. Be aware, Émilie, I don't want you to suffer. Make sure to protect yourself the best you can until you leave their house. Caetano is an awesome man, but he's weak. He believes all of Paula's lies."

The bowl with the leftover dye fell out of my hands. I felt like someone had just punched my stomach. My heart was beating fast, and my thoughts kept racing and bringing me back to what I had discovered earlier in the afternoon. I could not find the air to breathe. I resisted the urge to blow up in tears. The salon was full, and there was so much movement going on around me. I couldn't risk making a scene or exploding without being afraid of humiliating myself in front of high-paying customers or my coworkers. I didn't say anything to her. I wasn't able to formulate my thoughts or words. I bent over to pick up the bowl and cleaned the mess from the dye. I immediately left her sight.

The hair dye had to sit for thirty minutes, so this gave me enough time to collect myself. I went outside to get some fresh air and process her words. It was painful to hear her say this, but I felt in my heart that she was right. Her words resonated with me. I switched on my flight-or-flight response, becoming highly vigilant and back on guard. When I went inside, I grabbed a towel and returned to my client to wash her hair.

"Please follow me," I said.

She followed me and sat down in front of the sink. I grabbed latex gloves from the cabinet and took a deep breath.

"Thank you for warning me. I know that I need to be aware of the family, and I will," I said to her, my eyes filling with tears. I gently tilted her head back on the sink to prepare for her hair wash.

"I hope that Pedro will be the husband you deserve. I wish you all the happiness that I would wish for my own daughter. I mean it, Émilie," she said while looking me straight in the eyes. Her eyes had filled with tears as well, and I could tell that she was being genuine.

That night, Pedro was working late. I waited in my bedroom for him while the rest of his family were out at the community club. Around ten p.m., Pedro came home and saw that I was not well. I looked like I had been crying all day, but Pedro did not care to ask. He turned his face and walked out of the bedroom, avoiding conversation. This wouldn't have been the first time he had dismissed my feelings or ignored me, but that night I was not going to allow him to get away with bypassing me.

"Pedro, we need to talk right now," I said urgently, pulling him back into the bedroom. "Any time that we are alone, and I try to have a conversation about our relationship, you try everything to avoid it. Today, I've been crying, but you were about to walk away without even asking why or how I feel. We need to communicate with each other, or our relationship will not survive. The fact that you don't share anything with me, and you avoid me when I try talking to you makes me feel unseen."

"Well, I'm sorry you feel this way. But that's not my intention, my love. I'm not used to sharing my thoughts or my feelings, that's all. In my past relationships, I was not used to being open in this way," Pedro said.

"I am not your past relationships, I am me. And we need to work on this. Pedro, in less than six months we are going to get married. Our wedding date is set for August when my entire family in France will be coming . . . Pedro, are you even listening to me?"

I couldn't bear that he was preparing to turn on the CD player. He avoided making eye contact with me. But that wasn't going to stop me.

"You can see that I am trying to talk to you, but you just dismiss me like I have nothing important to say. You have zero interest in having a conversation with me. The only thing I ever see you do is watch soccer or play pool. Why am I even here? We have so much to prepare for, and you have very little interest," I continued.

I took advantage of this moment and let my frustration take over to discuss our dysfunctional relationship. Whenever I tried to speak to him about anything pertaining to our relationship, his family always interrupted us. Since Pedro's apartment was on the ground floor, people would knock on the window and call us to see if we were home. At this moment, I was determined to speak my mind to clear my chest.

"What do you mean, why are you here? You are here because we are going to get married. I love you," he said defensively, attempting to kiss me to distract me from our argument, but I shot him down and turned my face away from him.

"Sit down. We are not done with this conversation," I said to him sternly. Worried, he grabbed my hands and started to kiss them like crazy. I waited for him to finish until I knew he was listening.

"Pedro, your family is stealing things from me, and I can prove it. In her closet, your sister has some of my belongings that went missing. Your mother took my necklace and my bracelet. I know they come into my bedroom and touch my stuff. And I am almost certain that they took money from me. I had left twenty euros in one of my pockets, and now it's missing. I am hiding my money and all my valuables now. I do not trust them. We have so many things to buy for our apartment after we are married, and I am not going to sit back and let your mother steal my money, no way. Do you understand?" He was looking down at the floor like a dog that had just been yelled at by his owner. He nodded.

"I know, you are right. You can't trust them. I will talk to them. There are too many things that are not functional in my family. And now that I have you by my side, I can see it for myself. I cannot wait to get married and live in our apartment, just me and you," he said as he leaned in to kiss me.

Pedro stood up, grabbed me, and held me tightly in his arms. I felt some relief after our conversation, but I was not sure what was going to happen with his family. I wondered if Caetano was going to be made aware of what his wife and daughter had done. If Paula and Simona kept a lot from him, perhaps Pedro would keep this from him too.

# VIII

## MY BIG, FAT, CHEAP IN-LAWS

As I suspected, things shifted against my favour. Paula became problematic. Knowing that there were leftovers from the night before, I would come home for lunch and find them thrown in the garbage. Paula made sure there were no leftovers for me to eat. If anyone would call for me, she would purposely forget to write down the messages. She started directing toxic comments to her son and picked on his jealousy. She knew he had jealous tendencies, so she began to play with his head.

Five months passed, and my wedding date was approaching. I missed Anais and my mother so much; they had no idea what I was dealing with while living with Pedro's family. It was my decision to leave home, and I had accepted the consequences of moving out so soon. My doubts about getting married were increasing. Pedro was indeed a good guy, but he seemed to be under Paula's influence a lot of the time. Although he promised me that he would change, I hadn't seen much improvement on his part. In fact, I noticed he had started becoming possessive of me. He would randomly show up at the hair salon without telling me and wait for me at the end of my shift. My employers, Luisa and Miro, were co-owners of the salon.

One afternoon, when Pedro showed up unexpectedly and saw me smoking a cigarette outside of the salon with Miro and another co-worker, he lost it on me at the end of my shift.

"I don't like your boss. You shouldn't be smoking with him outside of the salon. You don't need to be talking to him outside work," Pedro asserted.

I was only seventeen years old, but who the fuck was he to tell me who I could and couldn't speak with? He even had the audacity to start picking on the clothes I was wearing.

"The skirts you wear are too short. Don't you see, you turn heads. All the guys I know are always telling me how beautiful you are. They always ask me how I get so lucky. But remember this, you are mine!" Pedro said in a dominant tone.

"You must be mistaken," I responded, feeling the blood boil in my veins, "You don't own me. I am not your property, and it is better for you to understand that. You do not get to decide who I should and shouldn't speak with, and you do not get to tell me what I should and shouldn't wear. I never gave you any reason to be jealous. A relationship is based on trust, and if you do not trust me, well, we have a bigger issue—especially since we are to be married in a month."

"I do not like when guys look at you. The skirt you are wearing today is too short. I don't want you to wear this. Do I make myself clear?" Pedro replied, pointing at my skirt with his little insecure index finger. I stared at him for a moment, and without hesitation I doubled my skirt on the waist to make it shorter.

"Pedro, if someone wants to cheat on their partner, they can be covered from their neck to do it. I am an honest and devoted fiancée. You have no right to act this way. I suggest that you work on yourself, or our marriage will never survive. I will not allow anyone to doubt me or my integrity," I responded strongly. Speechless, Pedro headed back to work, his break almost over.

I was so disappointed and hurt. Why was he getting jealous all of a sudden? How could he doubt me like this? These questions got me thinking . . . was he cheating on me? When people cheat, they begin to suspect that their partners are capable of doing the same.

That night after work, I decided to go for a walk around the neighbourhood instead of heading home. I had to clear my head. I had no energy to face Pedro's mother or sister. Caetano usually came home after nine p.m. every day, so he wouldn't have been home even if I wanted to speak with him.

I was confused. I didn't know if I should get married. I had a heaviness in my heart. I tried imagining all the possibilities . . . what would I do if I chose not to get married? Where would I live? I liked my work and my co-workers, I enjoyed living in Portugal, and I did not want to go back to France. But how could I tell my mom that I was having doubts? Family friends had already made travel arrangements to attend my wedding. I knew she would be disappointed either way, even if I cancelled the wedding. When I came home everybody was out, so I locked myself in the bedroom and went to sleep.

The next morning, I woke up very early so I could leave before Pedro came home from his night shift. I wasn't ready to face him after the previous day's argument. Having eaten my breakfast at a nearby coffee shop, I decided to head to work early. My boss Miro was at the front door of the salon, smoking a cigarette.

"Listen, child, I really care about you. You are a good kid. I believe you deserve someone better than Pedro. Thank you for your invitation, but my wife and I will not attend your wedding. I cannot witness what I believe is the biggest mistake of your life. If I show up to the church and the priest asks if anyone objects to your marriage, mark my words, child, I will object to it. You still have time. Tell your mother that you're calling the wedding off. I see your sadness, and I know you are not happy. You don't have to get married," Miro said to me.

Miro saw tears fall from my face, but he didn't entertain them for a second. He finished the last bit of his cigarette and went inside the salon, leaving me by myself to reflect on his words. Miro was always brutally honest with me. In a way, I saw him as a type of father figure in my life, because he usually looked out for me and always spoke his mind, even if I didn't always like what he said. But I had no words for Miro. I was conflicted. I wanted to believe that when Pedro and I moved out of his parents' apartment that things would get better.

Within a few days of our argument, Pedro apologized to me for his actions and promised to trust me. He reassured me that he would never question my loyalty again. I wanted to believe him, but part of me didn't.

A week before my wedding, my mother and sister finally arrived. I was so thrilled to see them. Anais and I caught up with each other's lives. She had started going to the gym after I moved to Portugal. She'd lost weight and toned her body. Her face was glowing, and she looked beautiful. When I had the opportunity to share some of my challenges living with Pedro's family, my mother immediately shut me down.

"I found out that Pedro's family was stealing from me. Paula started to play with his jealousy after I confronted him about their behaviour and—"

"What do you mean? What's going on? Why are you telling me this?" my mother interrupted.

"I am trying to—"

"Don't tell me that now you don't want to get married after all the money we spent on your wedding dress, and all the arrangements we made to have you move to Portugal. You are not going to make me go through another shameful situation like your father, are you? You made the bed, now lay on it!"

My mother was certainly a sad woman, but the older she got the more negative she became. She believed that not everyone was born lucky to be happy in the world. Our destiny was written and predetermined from the moment we were born. Some people were born to suffer, and there was nothing that they could do to change their destiny. She believed that she was born cursed, and her destiny was to suffer.

My mother's words echoed in my mind. I wanted to express my concerns, but she jumped to conclusions before I could say anything else. I kept reminding myself that everything was all going to work out. Everything was going to be fine as soon as Pedro and I got married and started living together on our own. I couldn't let my mother be more disappointed in me, and I didn't want to bring any more pain to her. I just wished that she would listen to me closely, and comfort me in how conflicted I was. I needed so much to be heard and seen by her.

Being her children, she believed our destiny was the same as hers. I thought of what we knew of my mother's story. She lost her father at five years old and had a difficult childhood. We knew that she was previously married to someone else before she married my father. She did not love the previous man and had been physically and sexually abused by him. She had a son from her previous marriage—though she never raised him, her mother did. Her son was a living reminder of the trauma she endured with her previous husband. That was all we knew about my mother's life before she met my father. We knew only fragments of my mother's life. I knew she carried a great deal of pain and suffering in her heart.

I had doubts about getting married, but if my destiny was already made up for me like my mother had always said, well, I guess I had no choice but to face it and own it. I just had to follow my destiny.

The gorgeous and warm August morning of my wedding day got off to a rough start. I wore a zip-up jean dress to get ready in so I wouldn't have to worry about ruining my hair. The dress was not unzipping, and I could not for the life of me take it off to put on my wedding dress. My mother eventually grabbed a pair of scissors and started cutting the jean dress apart. To top it off, Valerio was caught in traffic. Since we hadn't heard from my father after he left us, I selected Valerio to replace him to give me away at the altar. I was getting married at a Catholic church even though I had not been raised in the Catholic faith. Still, I always viewed churches as the houses of God. I always felt a sense of peace there. Pedro and his family were Catholic, and it was my mom's wish for me to marry in a Catholic church.

When I got to the church, I waited outside of the doors for almost forty-five minutes for Valerio to show up. The church had no air conditioning, and the guests waiting inside the church were feeling hot and restless, including the priest. Valerio's brother, Rui Sevilha, was next in line to walk me down the aisle if Valerio couldn't show up. Rui was also close to our family and was practically an uncle to me. In fact, Anais and I would always refer to him as our Uncle Rui.

"If you don't come inside in ten minutes, I will not officiate your wedding," the priest firmly stated.

"I'm just waiting for my uncle. He's the one who will be walking me down the aisle," I replied.

"If my brother doesn't come here in time, do you want me to walk you down the aisle?" Uncle Rui asked me.

"Yes, please, I would love to have you walk me down if he doesn't show up."

Uncle Rui put his blazer on and was prepared to walk me down the aisle instead. We had just started walking up the stairs to enter the church when Valerio finally arrived.

"Wait! Wait! I'm here!" Valerio shouted as he pulled up in front of the church in his grey luxury car. He parked and rushed toward us. Valerio was sweating and out of breath by the time he met me by the doors.

When I entered the church, the organist started to play the pipe organ and all the guests rose to watch me walk down the aisle. I could hear gasps and guests murmuring how gorgeous I looked, like a princess that you'd see in movies. The stunning white ball gown I wore was elegant, with puffy sleeves decorated with detailed lace and pearls. The back of the dress featured a necklace of pearls arranged symmetrically down the gown, open to show my back. The gown was perfectly voluptuous to match the shape of my body, and made of a gentle, light silk fabric that cast a graceful reflection in the mirror. The dress complemented my shiny blond hair and tanned skin. For the first time ever, I felt like a princess. At the end of the aisle, I could see Pedro's jaw drop as well. Valerio walked with me to the altar until we parted ways, leaving me with Pedro and the priest waiting to begin the ceremony.

At the back of my mind, I kept wondering if my father was going to appear. I knew that he was somewhere in Portugal. Was he going to show? I believe a small part of me secretly wished that he would stop the wedding, but the ceremony continued with no interruption and concluded when Pedro and I were pronounced husband and wife.

After the ceremony, the photographer drove us to a beautiful botanical garden in the middle of Lisbon to take pictures with our guests. Afterward, our guests made their way to the restaurant where the reception would take place. Pedro and I stayed behind with the photographer to have our newlywed photos taken.

"Pedro," the photographer said, "Émilie is one of the most beautiful brides that I have ever had the pleasure to photograph. She is truly a gem; you have to cherish her. You are a very lucky man!"

"You don't need to remind me that my wife is stunning," Pedro responded with an air of superiority. Once again, his jealousy was resurfacing.

"I see," the photographer whispered quietly to himself. Suddenly the energy shifted, and I could feel that the two of them just wanted to get these pictures over with. We had invited the photographer to the restaurant, but he decided at the last minute not to attend the dinner.

"Thank you for inviting me to dinner. I will have to return to the studio first to pick up some equipment. But I will meet you at the reception later on to take more photos."

When we arrived at the reception, everybody was hungry and waiting for us. It was very hot that day and the guests seemed to be restless, like they were at the ceremony. Shortly after we arrived, we asked for the food to start being served. The restaurant served seafood pastries, Portuguese vegetable soup, a plate of codfish, and a plate of meat. Paula's family sat on one side of the restaurant while my guests sat on the other. Paula's family barely interacted with my guests, and

I could sense tension and awkwardness in the air. The real party was coming from my side of the family. We could see people trying to get the party started with games and dancing. As the night started to wind down, I saw the owner of the restaurant approach Caetano with the bill. A few minutes went by, and Pedro walked toward me with the bill in his hand.

"My love, we have a problem. My parents have no money to pay for their half of the wedding. Your mother will have to pay for the whole wedding on her own," Pedro said, tiptoeing carefully around his words.

"Pedro, are you joking? What do you mean your parents don't have the money to pay for their half of the wedding? Our parents agreed a year ago that they would each pay half," I said to him, staring in complete denial. My mother saw my despair and understood right away that something was wrong.

"Émilie, what's the matter?" my mother asked.

I told her what Pedro had just dropped on me. My poor mother started panicking, clasping her hands to her face, and tearing up. She could not afford to pay for the *entire* wedding, at least not on the spot. I had a solution. I rushed to the gift box, opened all the envelopes in front of everyone, and started counting the money that Pedro and I had received as wedding gifts.

Watching me count the money, Uncle Rui understood immediately that something was wrong. I told him how my deceiving in-laws dropped the bomb that they had no money to pay for their share, and I was counting money from the gifts in hopes that we could afford to pay for the bill.

"Stop counting the money, Émilie," Uncle Rui started, "Don't worry, Maria, put your money away. Tell me what the total is, and I will issue you a cheque. You and I will do the math another day. It's Émilie's wedding; let's not spoil her day. Her in-laws already did a good job at that."

Uncle Rui gave me a kiss on my forehead and assured me that everything was going to be okay. At that moment, I felt like I had someone looking out for me. Indeed, Uncle Rui had money. He was a wealthy and influential businessman in the southern region of Portugal. Back when my father was around, he used to loan out money to Uncle Rui all the time. My father was actually the one who helped Uncle Rui start his own business. When I looked around for Pedro, my useless husband was nowhere to be found. I found out later on that, while we were dealing with his family's broken promise, he was busy smoking a joint outside the restaurant.

I was deeply disappointed in Caetano. I was not expecting this from him. From Paula, yes, she was someone who lied and manipulated circumstances in her favour all the time. The night of my wedding, I argued with Pedro. I could not believe his parents couldn't hold their end of the deal with my mother. To top it off, he wasn't even with me to take care of the bill situation at the end of the night. He dropped the bomb and left me alone.

"Babe, you had everything under control. Uncle Valerio's brother came to help. The guy is loaded with cash, so he can pay for literally anything," Pedro said to defend himself and justify his irresponsible behaviour. I could not believe the stupidity coming out of his mouth.

"Do you realize that the money he lent to my mother will still have to be paid back to him? Who is going to pay him back? Not my mother! Your parents will have to pay him back, Pedro. My mom will not be taken advantage of by your parents, do you hear me?" I shouted at him.

"I'm going to have a talk with my parents, I promise."

I always imagined a wedding day filled with beautiful memories, a day when everyone would be happy for me. My wedding night was not the night I had envisioned. I wondered if all the challenges of that day were signs that I shouldn't have gotten married. I no longer felt like a princess. I felt confused, guilty, and scared that I had just married the biggest mistake of my life—and my mother had to pay the price.

Suddenly, my father's voice echoed in the back of my mind: *You will always face pain because you are Satan's daughter. No one will ever love you. You will never be loved. You will never be anyone in life.*

He was wrong. I deserved love, and I deserved to be happy. Was I going to be happy?

# IX

## ADDICTED TO LIES

I had taken my vows in God's house, and I was committed to making my marriage work. When my family returned to France after the wedding, our vacation was over. Pedro and I officially moved to the new apartment at the end of August, the apartment that he bought a year before our wedding. It was located in the suburbs of Lisbon, so the commute to and from work with public transit took about three hours out of my day. Since Pedro drove and had shift work at the hospital, his commute was a lot shorter than mine. So, between the two of us, Pedro had more spare time at home than I did.

Pedro would not cook or do any housework. If I gave him specific tasks, like starting to prepare dinner or air-dry the laundry outside, he would forget to do it or pretend that he lost track of time. I'd return home after a long day at the salon to find that nothing was done. He would just sit by the television and watch his soccer games while drinking his mini bottles of beer. He came from a messy household, so to him he thought that the cleanliness of our house was good enough.

At work, Luisa and Miro hired a new girl named Ines to be the senior hair stylist technician. One of our previous technicians left for maternity leave, so Luisa and Miro thought this was the perfect opportunity to freshen the salon's signature and bring in newer and younger clients. Ines came from a well-established hair salon in Lisbon and was apparently an expert in the industry. She had a contagious smile, was short, and had brunette hair and beautiful brown eyes. She was curvy but fit and radiated an exotic beauty. The senior employees were not welcoming to Ines; they viewed her as a replacement and a threat to their work. Many clients loved Ines because she had wild energy, a positive spirit, and a creative flair for her highlights and perm-styling work. So many clients would come back asking for Ines that I wanted to see what the hype was with this new girl. I decided to give her a chance. After a few funny conversations, soon enough we started having lunch together.

Ines was normally supposed to start work at 8:30 a.m., an hour before me, but she always strolled in an hour late. My other coworkers would get annoyed at how she got away with being late, but as soon as she entered the salon they would forget about her tardiness because she brought a storm of wild energy with her.

One morning, the first client of the day had been waiting for Ines for almost forty-five minutes. I happened to be at work early that day, so Miro approached me looking annoyed.

"You, child. Pick up the phone and call your friend. We're all waiting for her. Ask her where she is," Miro said.

As I made my way to the phone, everyone's eyes locked on me, and I felt an overwhelming pressure to find out where she was. I called Ines's house, hoping that she would not pick up, but against my favour she answered my call.

"Hello?" Ines said sleepily.

"Where are you? Don't tell me you are still asleep," I murmured into the receiver.

"I'm on my way."

"You're on your way where?"

"I'm on my way to the bathroom."

"Oh my god, I'm going to kill you. Hurry up."

"I will. I'm probably going to take a taxi to work."

I hung up the phone as quickly as possible when Miro and Luisa started walking toward me.

"So where is she?" Miro asked impatiently.

"She said she's on her way."

"Jesus Christ, this girl is going to make me turn bald. This client has been waiting for almost an hour."

Her client continued to wait patiently for her despite Ines arriving over an hour late, but not once did Ines ever look at the clock to see if it was time to leave. She worked very hard and took pride in styling her clients' hair. Having Ines around made work so much more enjoyable that I looked forward to going to work every day. Ines was a single mother. She lived with her three-year-old son, her mother, and her younger brother. For the most part, Ines was reserved about her personal life. Without her knowing, Ines was my support system at work. She made me laugh and brightened my days.

One afternoon during one of our regular lunch dates, Ines decided to share her life story with me.

"I got married to the love of my life at sixteen. But I discovered months later that my husband had fallen into a heavy drug addiction," Ines started.

"Ines, I'm so sorry to hear that. Is the father of your son still around?" I asked sympathetically.

"Not really. He is so deep into his addiction that it's almost as though he doesn't live in the same world as us anymore. My son was born with an abnormality in his heart. He had to have heart surgery about five months after he was born. I left my husband after my son turned eight months old. I just couldn't handle my husband's addiction and my son's health issues at the same time. His mother helps my family a lot, but it's hard to be the sole provider for a child."

After listening to Ines's story, I decided to share some of my life's story and recent challenges with Pedro. The more Pedro sat down to watch his soccer games in the cozy armchair, the more he expected me to treat him like a child. After coming home from a long day, everything had to be done for him. I had to do his laundry, cook his meals, hand-wash the dishes, and clean the house. Slowly, I was starting to feel burnt out and distant. I could feel myself detaching from him. He never surprised me with romantic gestures. He knew how much I appreciated romantic gestures, yet he never brought me flowers or put in any effort to write me a card on special occasions.

We never celebrated my birthday with just the two of us—his Aunt Sara shared the same birthday as mine, so it was always a celebration of Sara's birthday together with mine.

To top it off, Pedro and I had recently financed a car, and even though I worked long hours and received generous tips from my clients, we barely made ends meet at the end of the month. Pedro and I divided our expenses. Every month, he was responsible for paying the mortgage, the building's maintenance fees, the car payments, the car insurance, and the gasoline, whereas I paid for the hydro, the telephone, the gas, the monthly transit pass, and the grocery bills. When Pedro had purchased the apartment before our wedding, he assured me that the mortgage for the apartment was connected to his hospital account. I never worried about paying the mortgage because the payments were taken directly from his salary. After all, Pedro was a government employee going to work regularly, so I trusted that the mortgage payments were being deducted from his monthly earnings.

However, on one of my days off, I received a phone call from the car dealership saying that the payments hadn't been submitted in over a month. It was almost time for the next month's payment to be submitted as well, so I started feeling concerned, knowing that we would be almost two months behind. I made my way to our bedroom. I kept three hundred euros stored inside an envelope that was hidden inside one of my drawers for emergencies. I unpacked all the clothes in the dresser to see if I could find it, but the envelope seemed to have magically disappeared. Initially I was upset, and I had a funny feeling that perhaps Pedro touched the money. I waited all day for him to come home from work to confront him about the missing envelope.

"Pedro, I received a phone call from the dealership earlier today. Apparently, you did not pay for last month's car payment. Do you know anything about this?" I asked politely.

"That doesn't sound right. I already paid for last month's bills," he said.

"Do you have the receipt for last month's car payment?"

"Uh, n-no. I don't have it here . . . I left it in my locker. I paid for it on my way to work."

"Okay. Tomorrow, would you please bring it home? I want to see it so we can call the dealership back and clear this mistake with them."

"Sure."

"By the way, you know that I keep some cash stored in our dresser in case of an emergency. I went there earlier today to look for the envelope, but it's gone. Did you touch it?"

"Of course not. It has to be there somewhere."

"Well, it's not. I even unpacked the drawers."

"I don't know where it could be, then."

"Listen, I know I didn't touch it. Nobody went into our bedroom. Nobody else knows about this stash except for you. Are you sure you didn't take it?"

"Your mother came here last week. Maybe she touched it."

"Are you serious?" I started to raise my voice. "Are you suggesting that my mother steals from her own daughter? You realize that every time my mother comes here, she brings us clothes and houseware. She helps with groceries as well. Why would she take money from me?"

"Well, I didn't touch it. If you're saying you didn't touch it, then it must be your mother."

"Why are you bringing my mother into this? My mother doesn't even know that I have this money here, and besides, she would never go inside our bedroom. I don't care if you touched the money, just tell me if you did."

"I didn't."

Within days of our argument, Pedro started to become visibly withdrawn from our relationship. He started to spend more time drinking at his parents' community club. Whenever he was at home, it seemed like he was on edge and always wanted to go to the balcony on his own. He started acting suspicious. He had no interest in intimacy, and, truthfully, neither did I. He was not caring for or treating me well, and I felt resistant to his touch. As I recalled the argument and shared my challenges with Pedro to Ines, she listened attentively.

"Émilie, with what you are describing to me, I think Pedro might be on drugs. I think you need to be on guard," she warned, her tone filled with certainty. "My brother is addicted to heavy drugs. My mother locks him out of the house now because he used to take things, like the stereo, the VHS, and even our jewellery, and sell them for his next fix. We never leave money lying around anymore because we know he will pocket it. If you are telling me that bills haven't been paid, and your envelope filled with cash mysteriously went missing, it sounds to me like Pedro might be on drugs."

I didn't want to believe her. I knew he smoked joints here and there, but he never *looked* high. I mean . . . was he? I'd never personally dealt with anyone under the influence of drugs. What did I know? I had a gut feeling that he wasn't telling me something, I just didn't know what it was.

It was February of 1997, almost a year and a half since Pedro and I moved into that apartment. For over a year, I continued to feel distant from my husband and struggled to pay for my share of the bills until I received my paycheque. Whenever my mother visited us from France, she brought clothes for me and offered to pay for my grocery bills, which was a big help at the time. Knowing of my financial situation, Ines would sometimes lend me some money.

On a late February evening when I returned home late from work, I noticed a note had been left on my door from the mail carrier, requesting a signature on a registered letter at the post office. The following morning, on a day off, I travelled to the post office to sign the letter. It was from the property management of our apartment, and it stated that we were a full year behind in paying for our building's maintenance fees, and soon we would be charged a penalty for every month that we missed. I couldn't understand how

Pedro missed a full year's worth of payments. At that point, I fucking had it. He was keeping something from me, and I knew he was lying.

Fuming, I returned before noon and found Pedro wasn't home. He had a shift in the evening, so I knew he would be returning home soon to get ready for work. This was the perfect opportunity to confront him on his bullshit. We were both distant from each other, we argued all the time, and we both had strong feelings that our marriage was falling apart. We didn't shop extravagantly, and my mother always helped us in other ways, so what was going on with the money? I went to the kitchen to make an espresso for myself. Within ten minutes, Pedro came home and sat at the kitchen table.

"Would you like an espresso too?" I asked.

"Sure," he said. I made him an espresso and placed it on the table. There was a momentary pause, but I finally found the right moment and the courage to speak my mind.

"Pedro, are you cheating on me? Tell me the truth," I blurted out, breaking the awkward silence. Pedro was caught off guard, not expecting that I would ask something so bold. He stood up from the table to help himself to some sugar.

"If I wanted to cheat on you, I would have taken up the many opportunities that I had at work. Nurses throw themselves at me all the time, but I would *never* cheat on you!" Pedro shouted defensively.

"So where is the money going? I just received a letter from the property management that our maintenance bills hadn't been paid in the last year. They're about to start charging penalties for every month that we missed. I'm curious to know about our other finances. As your wife, it is my right to know your finances. Can you show me the statements for our other bills? I want to see them."

I leaned on the marble counter while I was pouring sugar into a heavy crystal bowl that my mother had given me. Infuriated, Pedro charged toward me and grabbed my arm tightly. His arm was raised in the air as though he was ready to hit me.

"I have nothing to say! I don't have to show you, my account. Stop with all these questions. Fuck! Stop annoying me!"

I shook his tight grip off my arm and looked down at my crystal bowl, feeling my whole body burning with flames of anger. He stormed out of the kitchen but turned around to face me once more. Without any hesitation, I put the lid on the crystal sugar bowl and whipped it at him. He barely had time to duck, and the crystal bowl ended up hitting the wall instead, making a deep dent in the drywall.

"Pedro, this is the first and last time you threaten to hit me. I will *never* allow you to touch me. You may hit me first, but don't kid yourself, I will hit you back. Do you understand? Even though you didn't hit me, you still threatened me. How could you?" I erupted, angry and steaming. I was stunned at what had just happened, and his hands were shaking. There was a pause as I looked at him attentively.

"I . . . have issues . . . with drugs. I have been spending money on drugs and gambling. I am a mess, and I owe money to a few guys. I am not the man you deserve. I am sorry, Émilie," Pedro said shamefully.

It felt as though a trapdoor had opened at my feet. The world collapsed around me. Ines was right: I was married to someone addicted to drugs and gambling. I worked endlessly and still never had enough money. I was feeding a bottomless pit. I knew something was wrong; I felt it. But I didn't want this to be true. He didn't cheat on me, but this was betrayal. After he left the apartment, I spent the night contemplating what I needed to do next.

The following evening was accompanied by a painfully uncomfortable silence. I knew Pedro hadn't paid the building's maintenance fees. I knew he hadn't paid for some of the car's finance payments in the past. Now that Pedro and I were home for dinner, I was curious to see if the mortgage payments were still up to date.

"Émilie, the mortgage payments are deducted directly from my pay. There is no need to worry," Pedro assured me.

"I don't want to live like this anymore. You lied and deceived me, Pedro. You betrayed me. Why? Why did you get into this life?" I cried.

"I was always in this life. I just thought I would change when we started dating. You brought so much light in my life that I thought I could change, but I am not the man for you. I can't be the man you need me to be. I think we need to go our separate ways. We will sell the apartment. I will pay for my debts and what is left will be divided."

We agreed that this was the best decision for us.

The following day I contacted a real estate agent. She appeared to be in her early forties. When she asked why I wanted to sell the apartment, I told her the real story. She paused for a moment.

"First, I will need to check the status of the mortgage to make sure that everything has been paid up to this point. Do you know which bank your husband received his approval for the mortgage from?" she asked.

"I do, but I'm not too worried because my husband has his mortgage payments deducted from his monthly salary," I said.

"Hmm . . . okay, that's fine. But we will still have to check on the status of the mortgage. How about we go to your husband's bank tomorrow afternoon? It might be best not to tell him anything yet."

"Okay, I can probably extend my lunch hour and we can go during that time."

Without Pedro knowing, the real estate agent drove me to the bank the following day. When we arrived, I provided the teller with Pedro's full name and address. The moment the teller inputted Pedro's information, a red light reflected off his glasses and his face turned white as a ghost. I knew something was wrong.

"Excuse me, ma'am," he said. He went to get his manager.

The manager and the teller took us to a private room and hesitantly shared the news that my apartment was about to be seized.

Pedro had been behind on the mortgage payments for over two years. The apartment was already in the process of being repossessed by the bank. The news hit me like a lightning strike. My knees buckled in terror, and I almost collapsed. I could not believe it. The real estate agent held me as I started to sob heavily in her arms. She was asking the manager all the questions I was unable to articulate. The teller left the room and returned with a glass of water mixed with sugar cubes.

"The good news is your husband purchased the apartment before your wedding. The property is strictly under his name. Since this is an asset that was purchased before your wedding, you are not responsible for paying off any of his debts. You have nothing to worry about, as the consequences will only be on him. However, you need to evacuate the apartment as soon as you can. The apartment is in the process of being repossessed. At any moment anything inside your apartment can be seized and will be lost," the banker warned me.

The real estate agent and I left the bank and drove to work. During the car ride, I was trying to figure out how he could lie to me about the mortgage payments. He was a government employee, after all. It's not like he was working for a private company who happened to miss paying their employees. No, his earnings were stable and consistent because he worked for a government institution. How could I be so stupid and believe in him? I trusted him.

By the time I returned home, I still had an apartment to go home to, but I erupted with rage as soon as I saw Pedro.

"Son of a bitch, you lied to me! For over two years, you knew you were not paying the mortgage. I was paying the rest of the bills and taking care of the house for you while you were spending the money on God knows what. What did you do with all that money, Pedro? We are about to lose the house. Everything I worked for is going to be lost because of you," I shouted at him, but at this point, Pedro had barged into our bedroom and started packing up his duffel bag.

"You make me sick, Pedro! You are a liar! How could you put me through this when you knew everything I went through with my father? How could you do this to me?" Pedro rushed out of the bedroom into the hallway toward the front door.

"Get out! That's right! Get out! Where are your balls, man? You can't face anything, can you? Run away! Run to Mommy and Daddy, just go!"

He furiously opened the front door and slammed it shut behind him. I fell to my knees in the hallway of my apartment. All I could hear was the sound of my own sobs. I was furious and devastated. It was déjà vu. I had gone through this exact scenario with my father five years ago. I picked myself up from the floor and paced around the kitchen. A few minutes later, I heard the door unlock and Pedro opened the door with no shame on his face.

"I need ten euros for gas. My car has low fuel, and it won't be enough to get me to Lisbon," he said, emotion removed from his words.

I wanted him gone; I could not look at him. I gave him the ten euro note and he left. I felt used and abused. Before the apartment was about to be seized, the first thing I made sure of was that all my mother's belongings were collected and kept in one place. She had given me a grandfather clock, a bunch of silverware, a bronze mirror, a China collection, and other valuables when I moved into the apartment. I called Ines, and she came over with her boyfriend. I asked them to take anything valuable that belonged to my mother to store at her place temporarily. My family managed not to lose my mother's belongings after my father left us, and I could not afford to lose anything because of Pedro's addictions and lies.

I had devoted two years of my life to a man who only thought about himself. A man that had lost his ways and was dishonest. A man who lied continuously to his wife without issue. A man who took advantage of me and my hard work.

Was I following my mother's footsteps? Was I cursed? Was it my destiny to suffer? I was lost. I didn't know what to do or where to go. And I had no strength left.

# X

## GUARDIAN ANGELS

The signs to not marry him were there all along, but I ignored them. I believed I could find my happily ever after. Pedro made me believe that I could be loved. I needed to prove to myself that my father was wrong and that I could be loved. I gave my time, energy, and dedication to make our marriage successful and I had failed. I had wanted to prove to my mother and to myself that it was possible to have a happy marriage. Committed as I was to this man, I had failed. We were two souls that were disconnected on a deeper level. I realized that I couldn't share my heart with him, and that perhaps I was never truly in love, just in love with the idea of being loved.

The apartment was not mine. Two years of my time and personal investments were lost, but I left my relationship free of his debts. Sure, this experience felt like I was reliving the horror movie of when my father left us, but the difference was that I was free of the responsibility of looking after Pedro's money problems. I felt free. And yet I felt lost.

In the midst of the heaviest storms, when my life seemed to be dictated by chaos and emotional turmoil, I seemed to find a blessing from the hearts of others. When I met Mrs. D, it was as though God had deliberately guided me to a guardian angel. Mrs. D was the restaurant owner who lived ten minutes from the apartment that

Pedro and I had lived in. It just so happened that Mrs. D had a cousin who was good friends with my mother back in Chambéry, so my mother knew Mrs. D quite well. Mrs. D was a short lady who had dark hair and wore square frames. She was a little overweight, but she had strong arms like Popeye the Sailor. For a short woman, she was certainly strong. She could carry things many men struggled with. She lived with her husband, Mr. D, and had two sons. Her youngest son, however, was diagnosed with brain cancer six months after his wedding and passed away within a year. Mrs. D carried a heavy heart following her son's death, but she was still kind and compassionate toward others. I could feel her pain, but she found a place in her heart to feel mine as well. She extended her hand to help me and invited me to stay with her and her husband. Mrs. D was my saviour.

Mr. and Mrs. D were hardworking restaurant owners who lived in a gorgeous four-bedroom house. In the building where their restaurant was located, they owned an apartment unit directly above the restaurant that happened to be vacant. Mr. and Mrs. D offered to store all my belongings there until I could collect myself. They would not allow me to give them payment for the temporary space or contribute to any of the bills. They insisted that I live with them and save my money until I was back on my feet, and I was incredibly grateful.

On a night after work, Mr. and Mrs. D brought their car and met me at my old apartment to help me evacuate. They planned to make several trips to their vacant apartment to move my clothes and other small possessions. Since their car was compact, we could not take any furniture with us. We planned to lay all my belongings on bedsheets and fold them so they would be easy to carry and transport. We had no time to waste: the apartment could have been repossessed at any minute.

When I went inside the apartment, I noticed that some of the packing I had done the night prior with my homeware and clothes were missing, which meant that Pedro must have taken them while I was at work. I was enraged, angry as hell. A burning animosity erupted from me like a fiery volcano. He had played me for almost two years, not paying the mortgage, lying about it, asking for money, using me to feed his addictions, and now he was stealing my stuff?

On their third trip back to the vacant apartment, I had a moment to myself in my apartment. Surrounding me, I saw my life, my marriage, and all my hard work laid out on bedsheets on the floor.

"Why do I have to suffer so much? Why? I am tired of this suffering!" I shouted in the middle of the apartment.

Without thinking, my rage exploded, and I started to destroy everything that my hands could touch. In the bedroom I had shared with Pedro, I started slicing the mattress in different directions with a steak knife. I ripped the curtain rod out of the concrete wall with my bare hands and whipped it against the hardwood floor. Blinded by rage, I found myself in the living room. I shattered all the decorative glass shelves and the glass coffee table. I broke everything in sight until I had nothing left to destroy. I looked around me and realized that I was the storm that destroyed the apartment. The rush dissipated and was immediately replaced with a deep sadness.

I fell to my knees at the front door of our apartment. Mrs. D opened the door and looked around her. She processed the storm and understood what had happened. She kneeled and held me in her massive arms while I sobbed hysterically, rocking me back and forth and caressing my hair like a child.

"Émilie, right now you may not see this, but everything will be okay. You will be okay. You are free to live your life now. You have nothing that attaches you to him. You are free to rebuild your life. You are so young, my child. I know you suffered your share in this life but believe you will be happy, and you are going to find your way. You may not see it right now, but you will. I promise you. I am here. You can count on me. I am here," she whispered softly in my ear.

God, how much I needed to hear these words. Mrs. D was the soul who elevated my wounded heart. I longed for my mother to be the one who said these words. I wanted my mother to hold me. I knew I was strong—all my life I had no choice but to be strong for my mother and sister. But now I wished she could carry me through this moment. I wished she was there.

My mother was culturally conditioned to believe that divorce was a shameful thing to bring onto our family, especially after my father had left her. She was reviving the cultural guilt she faced when my father walked out. My parents lived a life filled with secrets and fake appearances, but I did not want to live a life of lies just to appease others. I was nineteen years old, and I knew people were going to judge and talk about me. I was ready to face the walk of shame.

I lived with Mr. and Mrs. D in their house for a year. I was so grateful for their hospitality. I cleaned their house regularly, I read books to Mrs. D while she was knitting, and we had a lot of conversations about our lives. I saved a lot of money while living with them since I had no bills to pay, except for my cell phone. At that time, I decided to get my driver's license. Once I passed my test, I financed my first car. It was a used car, but I knew I would be able to budget my money to pay off the monthly installments. Driving gave me a sense of freedom, and I loved it. I was no longer dependent on public transit or on other people giving me rides. I could finally go anywhere at any time.

In December 1999, it had been almost two years since our separation. Pedro and I finally finalized our divorce. An hour before our hearing, Pedro asked to grab a coffee with me close to the courthouse. As I approached the coffee shop, Pedro smiled when he saw me. When I got close to him, he gently grabbed my hand and kissed it. I gave him a kiss on his cheek. He appeared sad, and he had noticeably lost some weight. We got our coffee inside the shop and sat down outside.

"I wanted to apologize for all the pain that I've caused you. You did not deserve it. You were an amazing wife. You are all that I wish for in a woman. Please know that I loved you, and I always will. I am sorry I was not the man you needed me to be. Please forgive me." Pedro's voice broke a few times, and his words felt genuine and heartfelt. His beautiful green eyes were filled with tears, and my eyes started to moisten too.

"Pedro, I do forgive you. I did it a long time ago. Please forgive me too. I was too young to understand that I was expecting from you something you couldn't give to me. Please take care of yourself. I want you to be happy. I really do, Pedro," I said truthfully. He was holding my hand and gently caressing my palm with his fingers. He looked at me again.

"Ready?" he said.

I nodded. "Let's finalize the papers." He calmly helped me stand and we went inside the courthouse for our appointment. In less than forty-five minutes we were outside holding a copy of our divorce papers. It was bittersweet, but long overdue.

"Allow me to give you my last goodbye kiss," Pedro whispered softly in my ear. Smelling my perfume, Pedro held my head with his hands and gently kissed my lips. I wished him happiness and left. That was the last of Pedro.

A couple of months after my divorce, I decided to move closer to where my mom was living in Portugal. Tina and Valerio offered to give me their keys to housesit their summer vacation home in Portugal. They too were allowing me to live rent free; I would just have to pay for utilities. I bought Mrs. D a gold medal engraved with the message GOD BLESS YOU to thank her for looking after me. She was my guardian angel through my separation period. After my last meal with Mrs. D, I was ready to give her the medal and say my goodbyes.

"Mrs. D, I wanted to give you this small gift to show my gratitude for everything you have done for me," I said. I gave her the box and watched her open it.

"Émilie, the time that we shared together was the greatest gift to me. I've always wanted a daughter, and I loved every moment spent with you. I will miss our evening conversations. You are wise and kind. You are truly a beautiful gem, young lady. Your strength is incredible. I know you will accomplish greatness in this life; you just need to believe in yourself," she said. I gave her a hug and we held each other tightly for a few seconds.

"Thank you, Mrs. D. You have been my guardian angel, and I will always carry you in my heart."

A week after living in Tina and Valerio's vacation home, I found a job as a retail assistant manager in a high-end boutique in a small town about fifteen minutes from where I lived. Selling clothing to a more affluent demographic was not for me, but I needed to pay the utility bills, my monthly car payments and insurance, and gas. I was earning less money at this store than I was making in Lisbon.

It brought me some comfort knowing that the rest of the Sevilha family were also living close to me. Uncle Rui, Valerio's brother, was living there as well. On a Friday night in March, Uncle Rui and Aunt Teresa's daughters Margarida and Tania invited me to spend the night with them. When I arrived at the Sevilha home, Aunt Teresa and her daughters were home. They took my small suitcase and moved it to the guest room. We were planning on going into town that night, and we didn't know how late we would return home.

While they were getting ready to go out, I was waiting in the living room watching a Brazilian soap opera on the television with Aunt Teresa. The front door opened, and I stood up to greet Uncle Rui, who announced that he was returning home from an overnight trip. He smiled at me, and respectfully I gave him a kiss on both of his cheeks, a traditional European greeting. As I did this, he held me close to him and looked at me intently.

His eyes and voice seemed off—he was not his usual self. There was a look in his eyes that made me feel very uncomfortable, and I had never felt this way before in any of my interactions with him. Thankfully, Aunt Teresa hadn't noticed how he looked at me, but I immediately left the living room, went to the guest room, and tried to process our interaction. There was something very off with him and I could not explain it. Margarida knocked on the door a few minutes later and interrupted my thought process.

"Okay, Miss Émilie, do you want to have dinner with my parents? My father wants you to eat dinner with us. Otherwise, we can go out for dinner as we planned," she asked with her arm leaning against the doorframe.

"No, let's go out for dinner. Let's give your mom a break from cooking tonight," I replied quickly, without thinking twice.

I changed into a black jumpsuit, put on a light amount of makeup, and wore my black high-heel shoes. I was still feeling uneasy. I couldn't stop thinking about the way Uncle Rui had held me tightly, or the way he looked at me.

We made our way to the front door, and Uncle Rui was sitting on the couch by himself. I wished there was a hole for me to hide in. He scanned my outfit with a look of desire, almost as if he was undressing me with his eyes. My cell phone rang with an incoming notification. I looked at my phone—it was a friend texting me, and an idea came to mind. I did not want to return to that house. Fuck the sleepover, I did not want to be there. Something was telling me to get out. There was a heaviness, almost a sickness, in my chest, so I came up with a lie.

"Girls, I just got a message from my co-worker. I need to go to work tomorrow. I'm so sorry, but I will not be able to have a sleepover with you. We can still go out for dinner as planned, but I will have to head home right afterward since I don't have my work clothes here," I said, making sure Uncle Rui was also listening.

"Oh no! We were looking forward to the night. Are you sure you can't stay?" Margarida said.

"I can't, I'm sorry. How about we plan another day?"

"Yeah, we can plan something again soon."

I went back to the guest room, took my small case, and said my goodbyes to Uncle Rui and Aunt Teresa. As soon as I went outside, I could breathe again. What was that all about?

My parents always talked about how Uncle Rui had cheated on his wife. I've known him since I was a little girl, and I was like a daughter to him. Was something going on with him? Was I over-analyzing his behaviour? His gaze made me feel deeply uncomfortable, but I couldn't be certain. That night with the girls, I did not enjoy myself. I was up most of the night trying to make sense of what I had felt.

Two days after I saw the Sevilha family was a Sunday, and the boutique was closed. I received an urgent text message at ten a.m. It was Uncle Rui. He wanted to meet with me at a parking lot on the backside of a highway gas station, about forty kilometres from where we lived. He didn't want us to be seen together because we lived in a small town. He insisted that I needed to hear what he had to say, as it was very important. These messages made me feel uneasy. I was apprehensive about meeting with him, but perhaps this was an emergency. And the answers to my questions.

We met an hour later at the gas station parking lot, as per his request. I reversed into the spot in case I had to drive off. He parked his black luxury car right beside my car so we would be face to face. He rolled down his window and started speaking.

"Turn your car off and come inside mine, and we'll go for a drive," Uncle Rui said.

"No, Uncle Rui, I can hear you perfectly fine from here," I said. He smiled and took off his expensive sunglasses.

"Émilie, let's get straight to the point. I know you felt something the other day. You were uncomfortable around me, and I could see it. It was amusing, actually—you were once so cute and innocent. But remember, you were married before. Your innocence was lost, and now you are a woman. This is what I see in you: a vibrant, sexy, beautiful young woman. I want you, and I have a proposition for you," Uncle Rui said with an egotistical tone. I couldn't believe where he was going with this.

"You know how wealthy I am. I worked very hard to build an empire. I love my family. I love Teresa. She is the mother of my children, but she does not fulfill my fantasies and my sexual needs. I always had mistresses, and I always took care of each of them well. Look at you—you are all alone. You are divorced. Your dad left you with nothing. You work in a retail store and you make close to nothing. Why struggle?" he continued.

The more he spoke, the sicker I felt.

"I am ready to give you anything you want. You want to go back to school? I will pay for it. You want to open up a business? I will pay for it. You want a brand-new car? Just choose one, and I will pay for it," Uncle Rui said as he grabbed a pile of brochures and extended them to me across the windows. They were real estate brochures of condos and apartments.

"Look, Émilie, you can choose any apartment you want. I will buy a brand-new apartment; just choose where you want to live. I will give you anything you want, but I want you to be *mine*. Your beauty drives me insane. You can become the most successful woman that you want to be, but you need to dedicate three nights a week to me. Don't sleep with anyone else except for me. Most of the weekends, you will have to make your schedule free. If I miss you and I can find a last-minute trip on the weekend, I want you to be ready for me. We can travel anywhere you wish. I will give you anything you want, princess. You will be my queen. If you want to bear my child, I will give you the world and I will make sure our child will have everything. You make me happy, Émilie. I will make you even happier. I am good in bed, Émilie. If you sleep with me, you will never want to be with anyone else. If you agree, and you keep your side of the bargain, I will put the apartment under your name after a year. I am prepared to give you €20,000 in the next seventy-two hours in cash to start. I know you need money."

Every word coming out of his mouth felt like a knife mutilating my chest. He said these words naturally, as though this was a normal thing to ask, a simple business deal. My stomach felt sick, and my throat felt like it was starting to swell.

"You . . . you are my Uncle Rui. I have known you since I was little. I know your entire family! You are like a father to me. How can I even think of betraying the people I know and love? This is wrong, Uncle Rui. Y-you are mistaking me with women who you are used to dealing with," I answered with great effort. I could feel tears racing down my face as I mustered the courage to resist this sick man.

"Émilie, we are not blood-related. We are not even family. I kissed some of my nieces, so what? I am a man; you are a woman. We have desires, and we have needs. Forget about the family. When you are living like a princess, you will forget about them. You are divorced, you have no money, and you have no one to take care of you. Your father abandoned you, and even though he reappeared, he left you again. You are alone in this world, and I know that your mother is also financially strained. You could help her too. Émilie, think about this: in the next seventy-two hours, if you accept my proposition, I will give you €20,000 in cash. I am offering you a great deal. You just need to let loose and have fun. Just be ready to make me happy."

I wanted to punch his fucking face into the car door. Who on earth asks for this? I badly wanted to hurt him the same way he was hurting me. I paused to process everything he was saying before I looked at his sick, perverted face.

"You must think that money buys everything, don't you? That with money you can do whatever you want? I may not have money, but I am a young woman with dignity. I will *never* sell my soul to you, you get that? When I look at myself in the mirror, I want to be able to look at myself and not be ashamed. Never! I will never be your mistress! Uncle Rui, I had so much respect and affection for you. You broke my heart. What do you think my answer is?" Those were the last words I said to him. I had a knot in my throat that was suffocating me.

I quickly turned my car back on and floored it out of the parking lot. I accelerated at top speed, hoping he wouldn't pursue me. I was stunned, numb. How could he make such an offer to me? He was one of the only father figures I looked up to, and he wanted to sleep with me? How could this perverted man say those words to me? Do people with money believe that everyone has a price, is that it? Did he honestly think I would give in to his sick request?

On my drive home, I cried in disbelief. I struggled to breathe in the car, for I could not believe that he had gone to this extent to make such a sick request. The bastard knew about my mother's financial issues, and he was using it against me so I could buy into his scheme. How low could he go? I may not have had money, but at least I had values to live by, at least I had principles, at least I had dignity.

I am not sure how I made it home safely, but I did. A suffocating sadness crushed my heart, and suddenly I was reminded that most of the men I trusted in my life had deceived me. They were manipulative liars, and even perverts. I wanted nothing more than to feel trust because someone loved and respected me, not because they wanted something from me.

When Uncle Rui brought up my father reappearing, I couldn't help but remember the day of my nineteenth birthday. My father had shown up to the hair salon while I was working. It had been about five years since I had last seen my father after he abandoned us. Miro was highly suspicious of a man standing at the entrance.

"Émilie, the man at the door says he is your father. Look through the mirrors and tell me, is that him?" Miro asked me, pointing to the mirrors that reflected my father's image. He showed up to my work holding a massive bouquet of flowers, the most beautiful assortment I've ever seen. I thought I was going to faint when I saw him. I looked at Miro and reluctantly nodded.

"Émilie, I will be right there. I will stay close to you. Do not worry, he will not hurt you. I will be right there for you," Miro reassured me.

"Thank you," I said.

My father had hired a private detective to find me. He'd stalked me for weeks before he appeared by surprise on my birthday. He told me that he was living with a woman who had two young adult children, one of whom was a criminal. This woman had a criminal record as well, and she had been notorious for the falsification of documents.

"Why? After five years, why are you here? What do you want?" I asked him angrily.

"I missed you, and I wanted to reconnect," he said to me.

"Do you understand what you have done to me? To *us*? I would rather know that you have died and tell people that I had lost my father than tell people my father abandoned me."

My father was speechless—my words had punched his heart. But he still didn't give up.

Over the course of that week, my father appeared at my workplace every day. He even spoke to Pedro outside when he waited in front of the salon to pick me up at the end of the day.

One evening, the buzzer to my apartment rang and it was my father. He was barely comprehensible over the intercom, so Pedro and I went downstairs to see him. My father had been badly beaten; his face was swollen and bruised. Blood was running down his nose and his eyes. His glasses were shattered on his face and his clothes were stained with blood. I wanted to call the ambulance, but he refused.

"What happened to you?" I asked.

"The son of the woman I am living with robbed me with his gang. All my documents, my watch, my money, cheques . . . they took it all," he said.

"You need to call the police. You're dealing with dangerous people. I want to call the ambulance for you."

"Please, Émilie, don't call the ambulance. Don't call the police. I will go to the police station first thing tomorrow. I just need to take a bath and rest. I have no place to go. Please . . ." my father begged.

I looked at Pedro. Things between us were already challenging, but he supported me in whatever I decided to do.

"You can stay the night, Papa," I said, helping him out of his car.

I had every reason to turn him away, but in my heart, I could not find the cruelty to say no. I genuinely welcomed him into my home. I cleaned all his wounds, undressed him, and washed his clothes until I could remove all the bloodstains. After he was cleaned up, I fed him and prepared the second bedroom for him.

When I woke up the following morning, my father had disappeared without saying anything, but he had left a note and fifty euros on the kitchen counter.

*"Thank you and forget I was here. Here is €50 for the trouble,"* the note read.

That was the last time I saw my father. I wanted to believe that he went through all this trouble to find me because he loved and missed me. But, he only came around because he needed me. He used me and left me. He had broken my heart all over again; I was just a pawn in his game of chess.

The night after I saw Uncle Rui, I couldn't sleep. I suffered from a terrible night of insomnia. Our interaction brought up reminders of my failed relationships with Pedro and my father. I had nothing to show for my life at twenty years old. I disliked my work, I felt lost with no sense of direction in life, I had lost the ability to dream, and I felt so unhappy. I kept wondering if anyone loved me. I kept questioning my place in the world. Why did the people I loved hurt me so much? What was wrong with me? Was I bad, like my father always said?

I put my track pants on and left the house at two a.m. I drove along the cliffside roads overlooking the Atlantic Ocean, except it was dark and the ocean blended in with the night sky. The road was empty. It was a new moon, a beautiful night. The stars were shining, and the waves were crashing so rhythmically I could feel myself relax to the idea of death. If I died right now, would I be missed? Would it make a difference to the world? I was tired of the pain in my heart, tired of the suffering, tired of the fighting, tired of being taken advantage of. I could not find the courage to mistreat those who hurt me or seek revenge for how they treated me. I was tired of feeling this pain in my heart.

I peacefully closed my eyes and slowly let go of the steering wheel. I withdrew my foot from the pedal, and the car started travelling without my control. Surprisingly, I was not afraid; I was ready to stop the bleeding pain in my heart. I surrendered. At that moment, I heard a female voice whispering in my ear, "You have a mission here, my child. It is not your time yet." Her voice was angelic.

I was not alone in the car. A divine presence was travelling with me, I felt it. She pushed the car brakes seconds before the car hit the guardrail that separated the road from the steep cliff.

Slowly, I opened my eyes. I was on the side of the road, at the edge of the cliff close to the brink of suicide. The car stopped. I was safe. She saved me. I put my head on the steering wheel and convulsively cried.

I've heard this whisper before. I believed it was my maternal grandmother. It was a feeling in my heart. She saved my life. I felt and believed that God loved me and cared for me, sending a guardian angel to save me. I could not be certain that this was her, but I felt protected by this divine presence. This guardian angel rescued me, and she redirected me to keep on living. I was not alone after all.

I was not going to give up. It was not my time to leave this world. I had a mission. These words were pounding in my heart.

# XI

# THE CATHARTIC EXPERIENCE OF DANCE AND STORYTELLING

That night was a turning point for me. I did not know where my life was going to take me. I didn't even have a clear sense of direction. I stayed in the car for a while, purging all my negative emotions with a heavy cry. My body was shaking, I was trying to process that I was still alive.

That angelic voice reminded me that I had a purpose, one that I believed would soon be awakened. Since I was a child, I had experienced so much pain and invalidation, with deep wounds inflicted to my heart. The lifelong suffering could have ended if the car drove over the cliff, but it wasn't my time to give up. I needed to have faith. I needed to take control of my life. For the first time, I felt that I mattered and that I wasn't alone. I promised myself to never give up. I promised myself that no one would dictate my suffering anymore.

When I was ready to drive, I returned home safely and felt calmer once I laid in bed. The whole time, I had a feeling I was not alone. I knew that I would be okay. There was comfort in knowing that someone in heaven was watching over me. I just needed to have faith and believe in myself.

A few hours later that morning, I woke up with a new perspective on life. It was like I woke up that day with a consciousness that I hadn't experienced before. I was noticing the blue sky, the warm spring air, and the singing birds. My heart was filled with hope and faith. I believed that was the time to make a change that would alter the course of my life. I decided that morning it was time to look for another job. My work in retail felt unfulfilling and I needed to find something suitable for me that would bring me joy. I hadn't felt joy in a long time.

After my divorce, I started to fully embrace the social life of a young adult. I was embracing my freedom. I spent my time hanging out with friends almost every weekend. Through a few mutual friends of mine, I met a younger girl named Ana Julia at a nightclub in the summer of 1999. I was twenty-one when I met her, and she had just turned fifteen. Most of my friends were older than me or about my age, but there was something notably unique about Ana Julia considering how much younger she was. She was slender, with ocean-blue eyes and golden blonde curly hair that was full of life. Her posture, her body language, and the way she articulated herself all reminded me of myself.

Ana Julia seemed to be more of an observer. She spoke less and listened more. She was in tune with her surroundings and understood social cues. We had similar tastes in music, books, and fashion. She was someone very introverted. She was very quiet, not one to speak about her feelings or express emotion. Her parents were separated, and she barely spoke about her father. Her mother was working two jobs to sustain the household. It wasn't my place to push or ask her questions, and I knew she was reserved about her personal life. But from what she shared with me, it felt as though we had similar upbringings. We both had mothers who worked multiple jobs, we both had to become independent at such a young age, and we both had fathers who were absent from our lives.

Ana Julia was involved in the arts. She participated in singing and dancing competitions and was humble about her talents. Since the age of ten, she often travelled to Lisbon on her own to participate in competitions because her mother was busy working.

Hanging out with Ana Julia was delightful; we would laugh about the silliest of things and danced by ourselves in the middle of the living room. We spent our weeknights getting espresso from a café and our weekends clubbing together. We had a pre-clubbing ritual, where we spent our Saturday nights having dinner at home, followed by a sit-down at a café to socialize and meet some friends, followed by a drive to the clubs and bars along the coast. There were so many we could choose from by the ocean. We could hear the crashing waves whenever we stepped out of the car on our way to the clubs. I preferred to be in control of my night, mainly to have the freedom to leave the clubs at any time I wanted, so I never minded driving to our Saturday night outings. I knew many people would drink and drive when they went clubbing, but I never fell into that trap. It was irresponsible, and I never wanted to endanger anyone's life over a bad decision.

Ana Julia and I were known as the inseparable blondies when we went out together. We were well respected in the night world—we had fun but were responsible about it. We weren't the types of girls who hooked up with guys, drank irresponsibly, or smoked drugs for the sake of getting high. We were the type who went out at night to dance it all out. From midnight to six a.m. the dance floor was ours. Ana Julia and I released our stress and pain through the movement of our dancing bodies; it was like we naturally synchronized our wavelengths. When we sensed that a fight was about to take place, or when we became surrounded by an irresponsible group of people, we would look at each other and would just know it was time to leave. We wouldn't say anything, we just knew.

These moments were my therapy, my catharsis. I understood later on in my healing journey how important it is to move the body. There is enough evidence these days showing the mental health benefits of dance. There are studies showing the increased level of serotonin, the feel-good hormone. Through scans, it shows that our brains light up when we dance, improving brain cognition. I learned that energetically, there is release of the toxic energy trapped inside the body with movement.

Ana Julia and I allowed ourselves to be free, to follow the rhythm of the music and cleanse the soul, even if it was just for a few hours. Dancing brought a relief to my body that I looked forward to each week—it was cathartic to my soul.

It had been six months since I'd started looking for a new job and I still hadn't found anything. In September 2000, Ines told me about a private psychiatric clinic that was hiring caregivers. The job was based on shift work, which meant that working Saturdays and Sundays were mandatory, and working holidays was expected. I never saw myself as someone who could be a caregiver, but I decided to give it a chance because I didn't want to work in retail anymore.

While I wasn't too fond of the idea of sacrificing my weekends and holidays, I figured that I could use the extra money. I decided to submit an application to the clinic, thinking that perhaps this would be a chance for me to work with people living with mental health issues and psychiatric disorders. I went to the clinic to apply and completed an interview that same day. It was a fast process—they hired me on the spot under a six-month contract.

The psychiatry clinic was a private institution established over a hundred years ago, and it specialized in the psychiatric rehabilitation and care of patients living with mental health challenges. Sister Bella, the director of the institution at the time, was a nun. There were other nuns who were responsible for supervising and managing specific departments of the clinic. This clinic had specialized departments for female patients living with pre-existing and long-term mental health illnesses. There were departments specific for patients who lived with Alzheimer's disease, dementia, Parkinson's disease, schizophrenia, bipolar disorder, depression, and Down syndrome. The clinic also had a short-term inpatient unit for acute patients living with deep depression and experiencing psychosis, and for patients who were at risk for harming others or themselves. Usually, the acute patients were either male or female, and they would stay on a short-term basis until they were given the proper treatment, medication, and therapeutic approach. For all these different departments, the clinic had psychiatrists, psychologists, nurses, and a team of medical staff to assess and treat the different types of patients.

I was assigned to unit five, which combined chronic and acute patients on the same floor. The chronic patients were all women, living with schizophrenia and bipolar disorder. My role as a caregiver was to provide personal care and assistance to both kinds of patients. My duties included bathing and dressing patients who needed help, supervising them during meals, making sure they attended daily therapeutic activities, bringing meals from the basement kitchen, ensuring dietary restrictions were being met, and communicating with the medical team to report on their overall well-being.

Shortly before I started my position, I had to attend a mandatory workplace orientation to inform me of the different types of mental health disorders, clinical hazards, and workplace risks that I would be exposed to on the field. The only experience I had with dealing with someone who lived with mental health issues was my mother, who lived with depression for as long as I could remember. I knew that I would be undertaking a huge responsibility in my role, but somehow, I had no fear.

In unit five, the doors were always locked to prevent patients from escaping. There were a few incidents where patients attempted this, but they were mostly unsuccessful. For safety, the clinic needed to limit anything that patients could use to harm themselves or others. They were not allowed access to anything sharp, like shaving razors, scissors, writing tools, keys, or anything of the sort. In some cases, patients didn't even have access to their toothbrush. It was one of my responsibilities to provide them with their toothbrush and supervise them on their personal hygiene. Since I was working with patients who lived with schizophrenia and experienced at times hallucinations, I always needed to stay alert and monitor the patients and their behaviour, because a patient's mental status could change from day to day, hour to hour.

When I first started working at the facility, there were two senior caregivers there who had worked at the clinic for many years. One of them was not popular among the chronic patients living in the unit, as she seemed to be strict and authoritarian. This caregiver warned me to be careful with one specific patient named Felicity. Felicity was diagnosed with schizophrenia and was notorious for her aggressive behaviour. I listened to the warnings, but I did not want to fear or judge the patients.

Betinha, the other caregiver in the clinic, brought a bright, beaming smile and a young spirit to work every day. I could sense that many patients loved her. She was warm and respected throughout the clinic, and I preferred to work with her whenever I had the opportunity.

Two weeks into my work, I earned the responsibility of occasionally working alone. On a Wednesday afternoon in late September, after I had cleaned up the breakfast meals throughout the unit, I was assigned to collect laundry from the bedrooms. As I rolled the laundry cart down the hallway, someone accosted me from behind and grabbed the funny bone of my elbow, pressing it tightly.

"Give me a cigarette. I want a cigarette now, or I will rip off your elbow," she demanded.

I turned my head to glimpse who was behind me, and saw it was Felicity. The pupils of her eyes appeared constricted, and she seemed disgruntled. Calmly but firmly, I grabbed the hand that was pressing down on my elbow and tried to shake off her strong grip.

"Felicity, let go of my arm! Right now! Let go!" I ordered firmly; my voice raised slightly. Within seconds, Felicity let go. To my surprise, she leaned forward very close to me and laid her head on my shoulder.

"Émilie, don't get upset . . . I just wanted to see your reaction. I'm sorry. I will never hurt you. You remind me of my daughter. I promise, I will not hurt you," she said with her head leaning against my shoulder, her hand embracing my arm. I gently caressed her head.

"When I look at you, I see my daughter. She's about your age. You are good to us. I know you will protect us; I just know."

I was perplexed. What did she mean when she said I was going to protect them?

My direct supervisor, Sister Machada, had a strict demeanor and the management skills of a drill sergeant. She was sixty-five years old, petite, with white wavy hair and a long face, but she never smiled. She had minimal interactions with the patients, and when she did, she expressed no compassion for them. She arbitrarily punished them by removing them from their occupational therapy classes to do chores, and by limiting the patients' access to certain foods. In one instance, she handed a slice of toast to a patient without a jam packet. When the patient begged and had a tantrum to have a scoop of jam on her toast, Sister Machada immediately asked the nurse to have the patient injected with a heavy sedation for insubordination. Thankfully, she was unsuccessful in her request.

Unit five had a nursing station on the floor where the nurses were accessible and on-call for twenty-four hours. Some of the nurses were not very pleasant; we would only see them when the medication was needed or if we were dealing with an issue. For some nurses, the clinic was just a second job, so they didn't feel the need to push themselves at work.

On the other end of the spectrum, the clinic had nurses who were actually very sweet and dedicated workers. I established a genuine connection and friendship with Catarina and Beatriz. Catarina had short light hair, a curvy figure, and stylish glasses. She brought a contagious smile and a free spirit to work. We would crack jokes and laugh with each other. We would go for coffee together after lunch, and even invite some of our patients to tag along with us. She was very welcoming and seemed to genuinely care for her patients and her coworkers.

Beatriz had long dark hair and was tall with a strong figure. She was also very kind with her patients, but she was notably less talkative than Catarina. She was initially reserved, and it took a while before she finally warmed up to me. Beatriz and Catarina were more favourable among the patients. Even though Beatriz was less talkative, she had no issue standing up to Sister Machada. As a nurse, Beatriz had the authority to refuse Sister Machada's request to administer the patients with heavy sedation if she deemed it was not necessary, and she would do so openly.

By March of 2001, it had been six months into my work at the psychiatric clinic and I had grown fond of my work there. Of course, the responsibilities of the job never changed or got easier. I was still responsible for monitoring and supervising the patients. Some days were long, some were decent, and some days were more challenging than others.

Visiting hours occurred between three and four p.m. every day. During this time, we had to be vigilant around the chronic patients to make sure that they were participating in their activities and not wandering around. The most worrisome patient during visiting hours was Felicity. She was notorious for attempting to escape from the clinic, and she had to be constantly monitored.

The sad part about working at the clinic was knowing there were several patients who *never* had visitors. Many of the patients were older ladies, and they all had beautiful stories to share. We all have a story to share as human beings. It was painful knowing that many of their families had abandoned them or chosen not to visit them, and I humbly realized how important it was to connect with them, because as caregivers we were the only people left in their lives who gave them a human connection.

Sundays after Mass were the only time when chronic patients were free to do whatever they wanted. Whenever I had a shift on Sundays, I would borrow the CD player from the nursing station and turn on the music. The chronic patients loved it: they danced, laughed, and celebrated. I would join in on the fun too. I set the volume on low to make sure that we were not disturbing anyone, until Sister Machada decided to put an end to the Sunday music fun. She despised patients having fun and would find chores them to complete even though it was the responsibility of the cleaning staff to clean the clinic. Sundays, however, were the only days when Sister Machada could not assign patients to complete chores, so she would hide the CD player instead.

When I came into work at twelve p.m. on a Sunday, an hour after Mass had ended in the clinic, one of the chronic patients, Carla urgently, rushed to find me while I was walking in the hallway.

"Émilie, Émilie!" Carla shouted across the hallway. I turned around and saw her hurrying toward me. "We cannot have our Sunday dance activity; the CD player has disappeared! Now we cannot dance," she said nervously.

A crowd of chronic patients rushed behind her like it was the end of the world, all looking nervous and agitated. They looked forward to my Sunday afternoon shifts; I felt like the mother goose looking after her ducklings. I hugged each patient as they flocked around me.

"Don't worry, girls, I have an idea," I reassured them. "Like my Grade 9 math teacher always said: there is a solution to every problem! But first, let's have lunch." I led them down the hallway to the dining room.

After lunch, I gathered the patients and took them to the parking lot at the back of the clinic where my car was parked. I turned on my car and played music from the CD player at a decent volume. The patients danced for two hours, and some even did exercises and stretches. When I looked up at the clinic, I could see staff peeking out the window giving looks of disapproval, some shaking their heads. Most of the caregivers from the other units disapproved of what I was doing, but I would rather spend time with my patients than gossiping to other caregivers about them. A few of the nuns out for a stroll had crossed the garden to see what was going on. I was bringing a piece of heaven to these patients. One of the nuns smiled; the others hadn't said anything. We weren't doing anything wrong, and that was all that mattered to me.

In giving my patients a piece of heaven, I witnessed in them the same cathartic experience that Ana Julia and I felt every Saturday night while dancing. These patients were letting go of their pressure, their nervousness, and a little of their pain. They felt free and released the energy that was trapped in their bodies. They were present and living in the moment with no fear, no reservations. They moved their bodies to the rhythm of the music, and their energy was flowing freely and naturally with every song. In its purest form, their dancing created a sense of community with the other patients. Moments like these brought an overwhelming amount of joy and fulfillment to my heart.

These women craved love, compassion, and respect. All these women needed was to be seen, accepted, and cared for. Society and even some of their own families had labelled them crazy, incompetent, retarded, dumb, unlovable, or dangerous. But these ladies were much more than their diagnosis, they were beautiful souls. They each had a beautiful gift, a unique expression. They came from different backgrounds of pain and had experienced some level of trauma. They were kind and lovable, and like children, they needed protection. They sought love. Don't we all?

Of course, even when the patients were decompensated or had an outburst and needed a tweak to their medication, all they wanted was to be listened to. There was no better feeling than when I arrived at the clinic on my regular morning shift and saw a joyful expression appear on the face of each patient. Some opened their arms for a hug, some wanted a shoulder to lean their head on, some wanted to vent, some wanted comfort, and some wanted a moment of silence with me. It meant the world to me that they cared and held so much affection for me.

In the spring of 2002, after a year of working at the clinic, a young woman in her thirties named Debora was admitted into unit five. Debora was an acute patient who lived with a deep depression and had attempted suicide a few times. In her most recent attempt, her five-year-old daughter found her collapsed on the bathroom floor. Debora was a wealthy woman who lived in an affluent neighbourhood in the Portuguese Riviera. She had a husband and family who loved her and gave her an endless amount of support, but there was a deep pain within her that she couldn't explain. She was being treated in therapy and had been medicated for several months, but she felt at times that nothing was helping her. When she discovered that her daughter was the one who found her unconscious after her last attempt, she became committed to her healing because she did not want to traumatize her daughter with any more of her pain.

One afternoon during my lunch break, I visited her in her bedroom to see how she was feeling. I sat by the edge of her bed, and without asking questions, Debora opened her heart and shared her story.

"Émilie, I am trying to be grateful for all that I have, but at times I feel this pain . . . like a darkness within me. I love my husband; I love my family . . . but I just don't get it. At times, when the pain is truly unbearable, I convince myself that ending it all is the only solution, and I feel like no one is listening to me. Everyone keeps telling me I have no reason to be sad. I feel . . . invisible sometimes," Debora said.

I listened to her with my ears and my heart—not to give her answers, but to give her my full presence and to listen to her with compassion. I held a space for her with no judgement. Listening to her reminded me of the night I let go of the steering wheel of my car. It only takes a moment to visit the darkness in our hearts. When we immerse ourselves in the darkness, some of us are lucky enough to break ourselves out of it, while others are successful with the attempt to escape the pain. I shared my story with Debora, and the power of that sharing gave her a sense of relief. She related my story to hers, validating her feelings and the darkness that she felt at times.

Within a few weeks after our beautiful conversation, Debora left the clinic and gave me a beautiful bouquet of wooden flowers with a thank-you card. She wrote that I had touched her life and she would carry me forever in her heart. As I revisited our moment together, I understood that perhaps there is an immeasurable power in sharing our stories and listening to others with our hearts. When we deeply connect with each other and show compassion and empathy, our brain releases oxytocin, a hormone often associated with bonding that makes people feel warm and comforted. Often referred to as the "love hormone," oxytocin is released from hugging and human touch. By being fully present with Debora, it allowed her to share her story and establish a deep connection with me. Stories hold a greater power than we can comprehend. Exchanging stories has the power to purge emotions, awaken ideas, share feelings, and create a deep connection with people, but first it starts with *compassionate listening.*

All my life, I believed that with kindness and love we can change the world. I believed that love was the answer. It sounded ridiculous to others, but I believed it was the truth. My idols, Nelson Mandela and Mother Teresa, were proof of that powerful testimony.

I always felt connected with music and dance. Whenever I moved my body, I would feel a sense of release that was therapeutic to my body and soul. For the first time in my life, I watched some of the most wounded patients allow themselves to break free from their minds and suffering. Something as simple as sharing their story or dancing in the middle of the parking lot allowed them to purge the energy and emotions trapped in their bodies.

Little did I know that years after learning about the power of dance and storytelling this would be the foundation of my work with people, and an ongoing gift in my life.

# THE LIFE-CHANGING VACATION

It was shortly after my wedding that Anais met her husband in Portugal, later moving to Canada with him to start a family. I visited my sister in Canada when she gave birth to her daughter, Chanel. She had just given birth to her son, Jeffrey, and I wanted to visit her to celebrate the new addition to her family.

Ana Julia and I talked about travelling to Ibiza in Spain that year. We were interested in sightseeing and clubbing there, and we wanted to visit Ibiza's beautiful beaches during the hot summer. However, it had been four years since I had last seen Anais. We missed each other and I really wanted to meet my newborn nephew. As much as I wanted to travel to Ibiza with Ana Julia, I decided to venture off to Ontario to visit my sister for two weeks instead.

When I flew to Toronto in August 2002, my sister welcomed me at Pearson International Airport with my four-month-old nephew and my four-year-old niece. Jeffrey was a chubby baby; he was super playful and loved his food. Chanel was cute too; she was about to start her first year of kindergarten that September and was really excited to see me. Anais, however, appeared exhausted. I knew my niece had been having occasional temper tantrums ever since Jeffrey was born, and I could tell that Anais was finding it challenging to handle her during these unpleasant outbursts.

During our car ride back to Anais's house, it was agreed that I would be sharing my niece's room for the length of my stay, and I wondered how that was going to play out. As soon as we arrived at her house, my brother-in-law Enzo was there. On my last visit to Canada, I hesitated to be myself when Enzo was around because he wasn't very friendly. When Anais unlocked the front door, I left my bags along the side of the hallway and greeted him with the traditional European kiss. Afterward, he stared at me sternly and issued me a warning.

"Remember that this is my home. If there's something you don't like during your stay here, you can always wait for the next flight back home at the airport," he said to me in Portuguese.

"Understood," I replied. I knew it was better to say less whenever he was around.

My brother-in-law was charming, one might say. To ensure that I avoided confrontation with Enzo, I deliberately excused myself to go outside and have a cigarette whenever I needed a break from his strong presence.

The night I arrived in Canada I was suffering from jet lag after the eight-hour flight and slept poorly in Chanel's room. My niece would sleep with the television on and wake me up every two hours demanding a bottle of milk. Every time I returned from the kitchen with her milk, she would ask me to sleep on the floor because she wanted the whole bed to herself. It was bad enough I had a hard time falling asleep with the light from the television, now I had to sleep on the floor? It was like a circus sleeping in her bedroom.

An inconsiderate move of my brother-in-law: he made sure to schedule renovation work in his house the morning after I arrived. He was installing a hardwood floor in the living room, so by seven that morning we all had to evacuate the house. Who in their right mind would force his family—his wife, his four-month-old son, and his four-year-old daughter—to leave the house at seven a.m. on a Saturday? My brother-in-law.

When Anais, her children, and I left the house that morning, I noticed the dark brick bungalows with heavily aged appearances in certain areas in Toronto. They had an intimidating presence, a dark, uninviting front from being rundown and neglected for several years. I couldn't imagine myself living there; the homes were so close together compared to what I was used to seeing in Europe.

We spent our day travelling between coffee shops and shopping malls on public transit. After we spent several hours window shopping and aimlessly walking through malls, I could tell that the baby was getting fussy and feeling uncomfortable. Chanel wanted something from practically every store we walked by, and she erupted with an explosive tantrum whenever my sister said no. It was close to supper, and I too was feeling cranky.

"Anais, please, I can't take it anymore. I just want to go home," I begged her.

"But they are not done with the floors yet," she said.

"But the baby needs to get home. Count the hours—we've been out since seven a.m."

"Okay, fine, let's go."

We left the mall and took public transit back to Anais's house. By the time we arrived, the floor renovation was still not done. Enzo had two guys helping him. One of them was Anais's neighbour, who was working inside, while the other one was a younger man cutting wood on the driveway. I greeted him on our way to the front door.

"Hello, how are you?" I said to him.

He glimpsed at me briefly but did not reply. That wasn't nice of him.

Enzo wouldn't let us through the front door. He sent us to their neighbour's house instead. I felt so embarrassed; Anais's neighbour was not expecting us, and I could tell she was overwhelmed.

When Enzo and his workers took a break, we picked up Portuguese chicken. Everyone at dinner spoke Portuguese very well, so it was easy for me to understand them until they switched to English. I had learned some English back when I lived in France, but because I never practiced, I wasn't comfortable speaking it. By the time we left the neighbour's house it was past ten. I showered and immediately went to bed from the exhaustion of being out and about. It was another night of trying to filter out the light from the television as I laid my eyes to rest.

The following morning, as I was outside smoking a cigarette on the porch, the same young man who was cutting wood in front of Anais's house parked his large pickup truck on the driveway. His name was Tiago. Tiago had wavy black hair and intriguing hazel eyes and was reasonably tall. There was a mysterious tone to him: he was withdrawn in conversation, so it was hard to read him. He was dropping off some tools my brother-in-law needed. As he stepped onto the side bar of his pickup truck, he looked at me with a sudden interest.

"Hey! I have a question—I heard you really like espressos. Would you like to go to a very nice coffee shop downtown in a place that I know of tonight? I can pick you up at eight p.m.," Tiago asked thoughtfully.

I was about to politely decline when Anais came through the front door like a skyrocket with my nephew in her arms.

"Sure! That's a great idea, Tiago. She's going to love it. With the baby, it's so hard to go visit places with my sister. Thank you for taking her around!" she said with enthusiasm on my behalf.

I was going to kill her. I did not want to go. I didn't even know the guy. I waited for him to turn on the truck and drive away before I turned to give Anais a death stare.

"Anais, what the hell was that? I don't even know him, and I don't want to go! I came here to see you. Why did you say yes to him?" I snapped.

"Émilie, Tiago is such a great guy! He's honest and deeply kind. He has a car, and he was born in Toronto, so he knows his way around to take you to nice places to visit," Anais replied energetically.

I decided to bite the bullet and do my good deed for the day. I changed my clothes into something more casual, since we were just going for coffee.

Tiago was punctual and picked me up from Anais's house right on time. When I got into his pickup truck I caught a trace of his ginger citrus cologne, and it smelled nice. He wore a pair of jeans and a nice slim dress shirt. He brought me to a café that served the best espresso, according to him. And he was right: the espresso was delicious indeed. Tiago was short in conversation, and he stayed mostly quiet. The long silences made me feel tremendously uncomfortable. I tried to ask him questions about basic things without seeming inappropriate. I asked about the line of work he was in, how long he had known Enzo and Anais, where his parents were from, places in Portugal he visited . . . but he always gave me one-word answers and barely reciprocated. It got to the point that the silence was making me so anxious I started asking the dumbest questions.

"Do you see that machine over there?" I asked, pointing to a slushie machine filled with blue and red juices. "I've never seen something like that before. What's that called?"

He looked at me confused. "Uh . . . it's a slushie machine."

Of course I knew what it was. I was trying to break the ice, but it was such a dumb question. Any conversation I tried to initiate with him seemed to not work. He seemed a bit sad, but it was hard to pinpoint it. He was just difficult to read. When we finished our date, the car ride back to Anais's house was also painfully silent and I couldn't wait to return home.

As I made my way to the front door of Anais's house, I could see her peeking from the window, waiting eagerly for me to spill the beans. I walked in and told her about our awkward conversations during our painfully silent date.

"Jesus Christ, Émilie. What happened to you? What kind of questions did you ask the guy?" she exclaimed.

"I know, but I was so uncomfortable from the silence. You know how anxious I get when I'm with new people who don't talk. Is it just me, or does he seem to be a bit . . . sad?" I asked.

"I think he is—"

Enzo walked in and interrupted our conversation. I didn't want to discuss Tiago any further with Enzo around, so I went upstairs to bed.

The next day, Enzo invited many of his friends to show off his artistry, that was his hardwood floor! I had to admit it, the floor was beautiful. It had a smooth walnut finish and a glossy appearance. There was a small diamond shape in the middle of the pattern that was a unique detail. As I observed the finished floor, my sister was busy preparing dinner for the company that would be coming over that evening. Tiago was invited for dinner as well.

Tiago arrived, said a quick hello, ate dinner, and left soon after. It was an awkward visit. Anais and Enzo said their goodbyes to Tiago outside, and Enzo asked him if anything had happened the night prior during our coffee outing. Tiago seemed withdrawn the whole night. I had done nothing wrong to him, apart from making a fool out of myself because I couldn't handle the painful silence. But Tiago said nothing to Enzo. I started second-guessing myself and replaying our conversations from the other night in my head.

The following morning, Anais brought up Tiago. She could tell from the previous night's dinner that he was gloomy. He reminded her of Eeyore from Winnie the Pooh. She paced back and forth in the kitchen with the cordless phone in her hand.

"You need to call him to see how he is, because you must have said something to him that made him sad," she said.

"Apart from me asking a stupid question, I don't think I said anything to the guy! I was not disrespectful; I was very kind. I can't figure out what it could be! And anyway, most likely it has nothing to do with me. There could be something else going on in his life," I said.

"Just call him," Anais said as she pushed the phone against my chest.

"Come on, Anais! Stop pressuring me to call him. I did nothing wrong," I exclaimed, pushing the cordless phone back at her.

"Émilie, he's been through some challenging times. Trust me, he is a wonderful guy. Show some empathy! Just check in on him and thank him for taking you out."

I finally gave in and called Tiago just to shut her up. She forced me to put the phone on speaker. I waited, and by the third tone, Tiago picked up.

"Hello?" he answered.

"Hi Tiago, it's Émilie, Anais's sister," I said.

"I know it's you, I recognize your sister's number on the call display. And your French accent gave you away. I'm at work right now. What's up?"

"So . . . yesterday you seemed a bit withdrawn, and my sister has been bothering me, saying that I should check in on you. She seems to think that I said something wrong that may have upset you from our outing the other night. If I did say something wrong, I apologize."

"No not at all, it had nothing to do with you."

"Oh, okay. That's a relief."

"Yeah, no, don't worry about it. By the way, would you like to go for—"

"Coffee?"

"No, actually, I was wondering if you wanted to go out for dinner and drinks tomorrow night."

My sister nodded with excitement.

"Sure. What time tomorrow?"

"Let's say six o'clock. I'll pick you up."

"Okay. See you then."

I hung up.

"See? Was that so hard?" Anais exclaimed. I shrugged.

The next day, it had already been a full week since I'd arrived in Toronto. My trip was halfway over, and here I was helping Anais around the house with the kids to make the days fly by. I wasn't nervous to see Tiago again; he sounded like he was in better spirits over the phone.

When Tiago pulled into the driveway with his truck late in the afternoon, he was punctual once again. I got into his truck and saw that he was shaven and well-groomed. He was wearing black jeans, a casual black shirt, and cowboy boots. He appeared much happier now than when I had seen him the other night. He brought me to a beautiful, cozy Italian restaurant. He was much more talkative this time, asking me questions and appearing more engaged. We had a few good laughs, but I decided to be honest and tell him how uncomfortable I felt the first time we went out.

"I want to be honest with you," I started. "When we went out last time, I felt a bit uncomfortable with the silence. That's why I started asking silly questions."

"I noticed. But I knew that you knew that was a slushie machine. I'm pretty sure they have slushie machines in Portugal," he teased jokingly. "I felt your nervousness, but that day I was all in my head and I apologize for it. It had nothing to do with you."

"Okay, that's a relief. I'm pleased that it had nothing to do with me."

Tiago had the evening fully planned. When we finished our dinner at the Italian restaurant, he took me to a famous Toronto landmark, the CN Tower. He wanted me to see the bright city lights surrounding the tower at night, and from the top of the tower they were beautiful indeed. I observed the spectacular colours of the summer sunset while leaning against the glass windows.

Tiago left me for a moment to use the restrooms, and when he came back, he surprised me by squeezing my waist.

"Ahh shit!" I screamed when he grabbed me.

We both had a laugh. He was much more playful, and it seemed that both of us were enjoying each other's company. He took my hand and walked me toward the glass floor. I was afraid of heights—I could not look down without feeling terrified. I did, however, step on the glass floor slowly, but then immediately stepped back. Tiago laughed at my hesitation.

After visiting the iconic CN Tower, he took me to a fancy bar in downtown Toronto that had live music and talented performers. It had small tables and comfortable couches. Each couch had an Indian Motorcycles emblem embedded in the leather. Once we found a corner, we started getting to know each other. He spoke about his past relationships and his heartbreaks. He explained that he had bought his first house when he was twenty-five years old. He completed some renovations to his place and rented it out for a couple of years. He used to live with his parents, but after a few disagreements with his father he finally moved into his own place because he felt bad for putting his mother in an awkward position.

After listening to Tiago's story, I decided to share mine with him. Tiago was fully attentive when I spoke, and I could feel his compassion and interest. During some of the emotionally intense moments of my story, our hands touched a few times and it felt comforting. He had one leg crossed on the leather couch, and his knee was touching my leg. At times, his hand would make his way to my knee, but I did not mind it. The more I shared my story with him, the easier it felt to be myself. He had a cute laugh that I enjoyed, and I really liked his voice: calm and sensual, especially when he spoke in English.

We lost track of time together, and we ended up leaving the bar at two a.m. He drove me back to my sister's house, and when we got to the driveway we stepped out of his pickup and sat on the front porch until six. We kept talking without realizing how much time had passed. When he checked his phone, he realized it was time to head home and get ready for work. As I saw his pickup drive away, I felt butterflies in my stomach. The night had flown by, and the time we spent together felt like we were in another world. I could feel his genuine kindness. There was something very special about him that intrigued me. I made my way inside and went to bed for a few hours.

Tiago and I went out again for drinks that night, even though we were both visibly tired. We were happy to see each other. We talked about our lives, our goals, our deepest aspirations. It seemed like we were really getting to know each other. When we left the lounge, we went for a stroll around the city streets, and we laughed and joked in the middle of the busy crowds. We stopped for a break, and Tiago wrapped his arms around me. He pulled me closer; my heart was beating so fast I could only take little gasps of air. He stared deeply into my eyes, his own emanating love. His lips brushed against mine delicately, like butterfly wings, sending wild tremors along my spine. The kiss felt right. *He* felt right.

For the remainder of the week, we spent all our free time together. Something deep was happening—I was falling in love with him. He had all the qualities I looked for in a man. I felt protected and safe. He was educated, intelligent, and open to talking to me about everything. He was patient, calm, and deeply kind, but time was running out.

The day before I had to fly back to Portugal, he took me out on one last date. He drove me to Niagara Falls for a picnic on a wonderful sunny day. The waterfalls were breathtaking, and the mist was refreshing, I could see rainbows reflecting off the water. As we enjoyed our little picnic, we started to discuss the next step in our relationship.

"Émilie, I think I am in love with you, and I do not want to lose you. I have a house here, a full-time job, and I know there are opportunities here for the both of us. I know this is a lot to ask because you would be sacrificing your entire life to come here, but would you ever consider moving to Canada?"

"Tiago, I'm sorry, but I don't love it here. It's a different way of life. North America is so different from Europe. You don't have the ocean here. I love my job, and I also have my mom and all my friends in Portugal, but to tell you the truth, I also think I am falling in love with you. I'm not sure what to do."

For a moment there was silence. Tiago picked up my hand and spoke.

"I don't want to lose you. I will leave Toronto if I have to, just to be with you. I will do whatever it takes. I will even try to find a job in Portugal."

I smiled. I felt like I needed to grasp this moment with all my might. All of this was happening way too fast, and I knew I needed to make a decision—one that was perhaps going to shift the entire course of my life, but I needed to try. I needed to pursue what could be my happy ending.

# XIII

## LIFE ON THE OTHER SIDE OF THE OCEAN

The day of my departure, I left Toronto with a heavy heart. I asked Tiago not to drive me to the airport. I knew it would be too painful to say goodbye. During my overnight flight, I could not sleep. How could I leave everything behind that I had worked so hard to build for myself? I loved living in Portugal: the ocean, my friends, my job. And my mother—how was I going to leave my mom alone?

I arrived in Portugal early on a Saturday morning. My friends Alexandro and Bruna were waiting to pick me up at the airport. I had spent a lot of time with them after my divorce. They were close friends of mine and had been supportive of me over the years. I could not wait to tell them about Tiago and get their opinion, but I wasn't sure how they would react.

I was staying with Alexandro and Bruna for that first night because I was going to start my shift the next morning at the clinic. When I got to their apartment, Bruna felt it—she knew something was up, and I spilled the beans about Tiago. I was trying to process what had happened in the past fourteen days. I confessed that I was contemplating moving to Canada.

"Émilie, did you smoke something? Did you lose your mind?" Bruna said abruptly. "Please don't tell me that you are thinking of leaving and giving up your whole life for a guy that you just met? Are you crazy?"

She was right: it sounded completely ridiculous. I could not argue with that. Saying it out loud, it was even beginning to sound bizarre to me! But I had an inner knowing, a voice that was pushing me to try. I needed to try. He was the one.

"I know! It sounds absurd. But I can't explain in words what I feel. I feel in my heart that this is right," I said with uncertainty.

"This is going to pass. I don't think this is going to work. From what you've described in your last visits to Toronto, you don't even like Canada," she said.

Since sharing my trip with them, Alexandro had been quiet. When we were outside for a cigarette, Alexandro looked at me and finally spoke.

"Émilie . . . I want you to be happy. Please take the time to think about your life. There is so much for you to lose if you go. What if moving to Canada does not work out? You would have destroyed your life and everything you've built for yourself. In the end, if you decide to leave, we will still support you. But maybe think about this more carefully," Alexandro said.

My tears dropped to the ground one by one. I loved my friends, they cared for me, and they were like the family I chose for myself. Why did Tiago have to be on the other side of the Atlantic Ocean?

I started work at the clinic at seven thirty the next morning, and everyone was delighted to see me. Some of my chronic patients had even woken up early and were waiting by the doors to greet me. It made me so happy to see them. I had missed them too. I planned to go to my mother's house after work, but I was so nervous at how she would react to the news of my trip.

When I arrived at my mother's house, she was patiently waiting outside. She was so happy to see me, and she wanted to see the photographs of her grandchildren that I had brought back with me. We went inside, and I sat her down on her black leather couch to discuss my time with Tiago, since I knew it was going to come as a shock for her. During the three years following my divorce, I had been careful with dating, focusing on my goals and what I wanted to achieve. I once promised myself that I would never get married again or jump into a relationship too quickly. But here I was, having fallen in love with a man after a two-week trip, willing to drop everything to complete my love story.

As I explained everything to my mother, I felt guilty at the idea of leaving her behind. I started crying and began to feel as though I could not control myself. I was feeling like a bad daughter. My mother wiped the tears from my eyes and looked at me calmly.

"My daughter, if you truly believe that he can be your happiness, please don't worry about me. You go, live your life. You are old enough to understand the consequences of your decisions. I left my mother as well to live my life. Life comes to a full circle. It's time to live your life. Don't be afraid to leave me," she said softly.

Hearing her blessing, I held her legs and laid my head on her lap. I cried on my mother; I could not let go. I had no idea if it was the right decision. Nothing about love is rational, but I had a feeling in my heart that urged me to try. I preferred to land on my face than live with regrets.

Tiago and I spoke every day on the phone. We missed each other tremendously. The more I spoke to him, the more I knew I could not live without him. I just couldn't picture myself living in Toronto; the streets, the vibes of the city were so different. But I wanted to be with him.

A few days after I received my mother's blessing, I requested a meeting with the director of the clinic, and my request was granted on the same day. I sat in Sister Bella's office and explained that I was presenting my resignation. I would still give it to her in writing, but I needed to let her know personally first. Sister Bella really liked me, and I knew she appreciated me speaking to her about my decision first.

"My dear child, you are young and wise. You have a free spirit with a fire in you that I admire. You are responsible, and you have done a great job in unit 5. You stand strongly in what you believe in. You have a sense of justice, and you are kind. I deeply appreciate that in you, Émilie. God knows with no filter that you speak your truth and I respect that." Sister Bella said thoughtfully.

"Thank you," I replied.

"I want to offer you something. I truly believe that you will be happy with your decision, but in the circumstance that you want to come back, I am willing to leave your position open for six months. We will find someone to cover it temporarily, but I will keep your job open for you if you decide to come back."

"Sister Bella, thank you so much. I am so grateful. You are giving me the gift of time. If there is anything I can do before I leave, please let me know."

"Blessings my child. It is my pleasure to do this for you. I believe that you will be very happy."

Nurses, doctors, and acute patients had given her amazing feedback about my performance. Her reassurance brought me a sense of ease. If I needed to come back to Portugal, I had a job waiting for me.

By September, I had to sell my car and find someone to carry the rest of my car payments, and it seemed that Alexandro was willing to help me with that. My French passport was already in the process of being renewed so I could book my ticket to leave for Toronto. October 4, 2002 was the day that I would be leaving my life behind to join Tiago and my sister in Toronto.

Between packing, tying up loose ends, and collecting all the paperwork needed to move to Canada, the rest of the month was quite busy. My luggage could only weigh so much, so I essentially had to pack my entire life in a 50 kg luggage bag. Ana Julia, Catarina, Beatriz, and Ines were surprised with my decision. I could feel their hesitation. It was a lot for them to take in at once, but, as always, their support prevailed.

When it was time to share the news with my chronic patients, they were all devastated. They did not want to see me leave. I had created meaningful relationships with these women, and I cared about them deeply. Right before I left, Betinha and the ladies of the clinic threw a small celebration for me in the cafeteria. Saying goodbye to everybody was difficult, and Betinha had been like a mother to me. She looked after me like her own daughter during the two years that I was at the clinic.

Beatriz and Catarina had prepared a special evening for me four days before my departure. They decided to treat me to a modern-style Italian restaurant that was close to the coastline. I was sitting in the backseat of Catarina's car on our way to the restaurant. But before we stepped out of the car, they turned around and Beatriz extended a jewellery box with a card wrapped under it.

"Girls, what is this? It's not my birthday!" I said, feeling grateful and surprised.

"We know, Émilie. We wanted to give you something that you could take with you, and it's something we thought of that would keep us close to your heart. Please don't forget us," Beatriz said, her voice cracking. Catarina had already started to tear up.

I opened the box. They had gifted me a beautiful sterling silver watch. I clasped my hand to my face out of joy, wiping a teardrop from my cheek. These ladies had never looked down on me or looked at me as anything less during our time at the clinic. We had so much respect for each other, and they taught me an enormous amount about caring for patients. I carried a sparkling energy with me during the time I spent with patients, and it made Catarina and Beatriz's work easier at times, because the patients trusted me.

After we had our dinner, the three of us went to a bar by the beach. I took in the smell of the Atlantic Ocean and observed the stars of the night sky with my friends. It was one of the most precious goodbyes. There is a Portuguese saying: *"recorder è viver."* That translates to, "Remembering is living." I will remember this moment for the rest of my life.

When Catarina and Beatriz dropped me off in front of my house, I placed a hand on their shoulders.

"Catarina and Beatriz, thank you for your friendship. It is the most beautiful gift to me, and it is an honour to have worked with both of you. I will always be here for you, and I will always carry you both in my heart. I promise. My door will always be open for you. If you ever take a trip to Canada, please come visit me in Toronto," I said.

"We will definitely keep in touch. We are going to miss you," Beatriz said.

"Well, we have a house in Toronto now! So we can visit," Catarina said jokingly, her eyes filled with tears.

Two days before I left, it was time to say my goodbyes to Ana Julia. Like usual, I picked her up from her apartment. To my surprise, she was already waiting for me at her building door. Usually, I had to wait for her to come out. We decided to go to our favourite bar, located right on the beach. It had been a few weeks since we had last seen each other.

Ana Julia was studying finances in Lisbon and had met a guy. They were not officially dating, but she liked him. Ana Julia had always been introverted. She did not know how to express her emotions and had kept her deep sadness and pain to herself until we found each other. For the first time in her life, she had allowed herself to take her walls down and trust me. She had allowed herself to feel emotions and share them with someone else without fear. She had allowed me to hold her in my arms and reciprocate my affection.

She had given me the key to the castle of her deepest feelings. I was the first person who showed her affection by simply hugging her and holding her in my arms. I was the first person who created a space for her that no one else ever gave her—a space to be seen, heard, understood, and loved. Ana Julia learned that there were people in the world who genuinely cared without any agenda. Ana Julia learned the power of love.

We were connected by the same pain. We lacked love and acceptance from our fathers. We felt unseen, unheard, and unloved, but our friendship was a tremendous gift to us. Just like me, Ana Julia had been abandoned. That was why it was so difficult for me to say goodbye to her. When I contemplated what my purpose was after my suicide attempt three years ago, I started to believe that perhaps my purpose was to open my heart to others, including my patients, my mother, and, of course, Ana Julia. Ana Julia had given me a sense of purpose and belonging. I wanted her to know that I would never abandon her. Even though I was going to be physically absent, I would always be present in her life.

"Ana Julia, listen, baby girl. I will always be here for you. When you miss me and your heart is tight, look at the night sky. The star that shines the brightest will be me. When you close your eyes you will feel me, and I will always be with you, even if I am not physically here. I promise," I said to her.

"This is one of the most difficult days of my life, Émilie. Saying goodbye to you is ripping my heart apart. You are my best friend, my sister. Even though we will be apart, I know in my heart that you will never abandon me. You are going to be there for me always, just like I will for you," Ana Julia said as a tear dropped from her cheek.

We hugged each other and looked up at the night sky. She was silently crying. Our drive back to her apartment was filled with a deep silence. She kept squeezing my hand on the gearshift. She did not want to let me go, she did not want to say goodbye, and neither did I. When the night came to an end, my heart was hurting as we shared our last goodbye.

When I got home, I found my mother watching television while waiting for me to return. We were going to spend one last night together at her house. We made ourselves tea and sat down on the couch.

"Ah, Émilie, now I am alone, completely alone. You are leaving, and I will have no one anymore," my mother said with an uneasy and sad tone.

I laid my head on her lap, exchanging tears and feeling a tremendous amount of guilt. I should not leave her alone. What kind of a daughter leaves her mother alone? What would she do if she needed help? Who would help her? These thoughts raced through my mind. We talked and watched television for a couple of hours, but the time flew, and I started to feel sleepy. I went to bed and silently cried myself to sleep. I could hear my mother crying in the other room by herself.

The following morning, I finally finished packing. I had to compact the last seven years of my life in Portugal into four sports bags, leaving behind a lot of clothes, memories, and bibelots that I couldn't bring with me. My mother was silent. I felt like the worst daughter in the world, bringing her the pain that she was feeling. I felt incredibly guilty, unsure whether I had made the right decision or not. I knew I made a fast decision, yet I still couldn't tell if it was impulsive or the right one, even though it felt right. My father's words replayed in my head: "You are the Devil's child. You will never be happy."

Before I drove off to Alexandro and Bruna's apartment in Lisbon, I asked the neighbour if she could stay with my mother, just to make sure she wasn't alone.

"Maman, very soon you are coming to visit us, right? In the blink of an eye, you will be with us again," I said to her.

"Yes, my daughter. Please drive safely. Call me when you get to the airport," she said.

"Je t'aime, ma petite maman."

"Je t'aime, Émilie."

Her eyes were filled with sadness as she watched me drive away.

I stayed the night at Alexandro and Bruna's apartment and gave Alexandro the keys to my car to sell it on my behalf. On October 4, the following morning, Alexandro and Bruna dropped me off at the airport in Lisbon.

I checked my bags at the airport and waited an hour before my eight-hour flight to Toronto. My flight was filled with mixed emotions, excitement, guilt, happiness, confusion, and a pain in my heart. My mind was battling with my heart, figuring out if I had made the right decision. There were several moments of doubt when I thought I was making a huge mistake. In these moments, I wanted the plane to turn back. But my heart kept telling me to look forward to the new beginning ahead.

The plane landed at Pearson International Airport, and finally I arrived in Toronto. I went through customs, picked up my sports bags from the conveyor belt, and stood before the sliding doors of Terminal 3.

*This is it, Émilie. You are starting a new adventure. May Tiago be the one you have been waiting for. Please, God.*

The sliding doors opened and there he was, waiting for me.

# XIV

## GEOGRAPHICALLY DISPLACED

"Thank you for trusting. I love you, Émilie," he whispered in my ear as soon as we were together again.

Tiago carried my four heavy bags to his truck and we made our way back to his house. He lived in a one-bedroom red-brick bungalow with a huge backyard. He needed to renovate many things in the house. He was determined at some point to extend the house, and he had enough land to do so.

We had decided to live together. I figured that the best way to know if Tiago was the one was to live with him first. After I settled my stuff in his house, Tiago took me out to a small traditional Portuguese restaurant where he knew the owners. He was so proud to introduce me as his girlfriend to them. But as soon as Tiago and the owners switched to English, I felt lost. I felt embarrassed that I couldn't understand them.

Everything seemed surreal. I felt like I was nowhere—not in Portugal, not in Canada. My body was there, but I was not. It was a weird sensation where I felt completely out of balance. I felt like I needed to rest and reground.

Over the next few days, Tiago invited me to decorate the house to make me feel more at home. He took a few days off work to be with me. Together, we put up picture frames and displayed a few decorative pieces that I had brought from Portugal that were meaningful to me. Tiago brought me to a supermarket and let me choose any food that I wanted from the shelves. As anxious as I was living in a new country, he welcomed me warmly into his life and home.

Tiago wanted me to meet his mother for the very first time, but his parents were in Portugal when I arrived. My sister was over the moon to have me live here in Canada with her. Her house was close to mine, so it was convenient to walk to her place and have lunch with her while Enzo was at work. Since school had started for Chanel, I volunteered to watch Jeffrey for Anais during the day while she went to run some errands. I felt more involved in my sister's life again, and it was refreshing to be close to my niece and nephew.

A few weeks passed, and Tiago's parents finally returned home from Portugal. I was excited and nervous to meet his mother. When we picked her up to go for a coffee, I came out of the car to greet his mother. To Tiago's own surprise, his mother greeted me with a smile and gave me a welcoming hug. His mother was kind. She had wavy snow-white hair, a beautiful smile, and many traits that were passed down to Tiago. She was calm and seemed very patient. Tiago once mentioned that his mother was very quiet, but that evening when we went to the coffee shop she was very talkative and took an interest in getting to know me.

"Tiago, you need to introduce Émilie to your father," she said. She reached over to hold my hand. "You need to take Tiago back to my home. He needs to speak with his father again. He needs to forget about what happened between him and his father. It would make me very happy if they reconnected."

"I really want to meet Tiago's father, and I think it's time to make peace. This is a new chapter in our lives," I assured her.

Tiago hadn't been on speaking terms with his father for several months, and his mother was suffering from it. I really liked her. She made me feel so welcome. We brought her home, and she gave me another big hug before she walked to the front door. I felt as though his mother was giving us her blessing.

A week passed, and Tiago finally agreed to visit his father. I felt apprehensive. I knew he wasn't too keen on visiting his father after ten long months of not speaking to him.

When we went to his parents' house, his mother welcomed us at the door, her eyes filling with tears because her son was finally coming back home. Tiago's father was sitting at the head of the kitchen table. He was a short man with white hair and a firm posture. Tiago shook his hand while his father remained sitting and introduced me as his girlfriend. His father did not stand for Tiago, but he stood up to welcome me. The tension was real—Tiago was nervous, and his mother was worried that a heated disagreement would unfold. His mother prepared a roast. The room was filled with silence and the sound of clinking dinnerware. As per usual, the silence made me feel anxious. To break the ice, I decided to start up a conversation.

"Do you like to watch soccer?" I asked Tiago's father.

He responded with a nod.

"My favourite team is Sporting Lisbon. What's yours?" I asked.

He looked at me annoyed.

"Benfica," he said briefly.

Fantastic. These were rival teams in Portugal. I attempted to make a few jokes and a few other icebreakers, but eventually I knew to give up. I wanted to kill Tiago because I could see him snickering while watching my failed attempts. It was a short dinner visit, but thankfully Tiago was reconnecting with his father, and I was pleased to see that his mother was happy. She was such a sweet soul.

By November, the air in Toronto had dropped to such cold temperatures that it was already colder than our worst winter days in Lisbon. The most painful part about this Canadian weather was that there were many cloudy days and no sun. I decided that this would be the best time to quit smoking cigarettes, since it was too cold to go outside.

Although I was happy to be with Tiago, I cried every day. Staying at home was taking a toll on me. I missed my mother, my friends, and my work tremendously. Tiago would come home from work and be greeted by my swollen and puffy eyes. I tried to hide my tears and my emotions from him, but my face was too expressive. Tiago felt bad, but he understood that this was a culture shock for me.

The worst part about being in Canada was that I couldn't express myself in English. I had always been independent in my French and Portuguese tongue. But for the first time in my life, I had to depend on someone else to communicate on my behalf. Tiago had to translate everything that was directed to me. My self-esteem was brought down, and it made me feel uncomfortable. I felt like I was losing more and more of my identity with each passing day. I knew that I needed to get out of the house to distract me from feeling this way. I knew that I had to start working, but without a work visa and a social insurance number, this was not possible.

A good friend of mine back in Portugal had a sister named Lily who was married and living in Toronto. Lily was building a gorgeous house in Portugal and was living in Canada temporarily until their dream house in Portugal was done. She lived and cleaned houses with her mother-in-law. Lily would sometimes invite me to spend the day with her, so I could get out a little. She missed her family and friends tremendously, and just like me she was geographically misplaced and homesick. She understood perfectly how I felt.

On a Friday afternoon in mid-November, Tiago surprised me with a weekend getaway.

"Émilie, this weekend I am taking you somewhere I believe you will love," Tiago said with enthusiasm. "I know being here has been difficult for you. You are probably not used to the cold winters here. I want to give you the world you deserve."

My heart melted. Even though I hated the climate and lifestyle in Toronto, Tiago showed great devotion to easing my transition.

"Okay. I'm looking forward to what you have in store for me," I said. I was excited to get out of the house.

The following Saturday morning, Tiago and I woke up early and left after breakfast. I had no clue where he was taking me. After an hour's drive, we arrived at a beautiful town in Southern Ontario known as Niagara-on-the-Lake. This little town was known for their wine-tasting tours and historic nineteenth-century buildings. Although it was colder here than it was in Toronto, the town had a lovely lakeside atmosphere.

Tiago had reserved a room in a vintage Victorian-style hotel that was luxurious and beautiful. Our room had a four-poster king-size bed, with fancy drapery dangling from each post. The room was furnished with a beautiful loveseat, a well-crafted dresser, and fancy end tables. The paintings in the room were still-life images of everyday life in the nineteenth century.

After taking in the atmosphere of the hotel, Tiago and I decided to walk along the stony path around the hotel. We walked toward a large stone at the corner of the path, and we finally came to a stop where we had a clear view of the garden.

"Émilie, please sit down," Tiago asked softly.

I was not properly dressed for the weather. I'd worn a thin black leather jacket that was not suitable for the Canadian cold. I shivered at the idea of sitting on the cold rock before us.

"No, thank you, I am fine," I replied.

"Please, Émilie, just sit down on this rock and enjoy the scenery."

"Nope, I am fine. Let's continue walking around because I'm freezing. The walking distracts me from the cold air."

"Please, Émilie, for two minutes, just sit down," Tiago said with an insistent tone.

I finally caved to his request and sat on the stone, but my body became chilled instantly and I did not like this feeling.

Tiago fell on one knee and, to my surprise, reached out and grabbed my hand.

"Do you want to marry me? I don't have a ring yet, but I felt that this was the right moment to ask you to marry me because I want to spend the rest of my life with you."

"Yes! Yes! I will!" I shouted. He stood up from the ground and passionately kissed me in the cold November afternoon.

He seized the moment with his two hands, and I accepted. I had always said to myself that I did not want to marry again, but in my heart I knew that Tiago was the one. Even though I was not living back at home in Portugal, I knew that I had found someone I could grow old with and be happy with for the rest of my life. I loved him so much.

We had a wonderful breakfast at the hotel's restaurant the following morning. They had set up a gourmet buffet, serving omelettes, pancakes, croissants, fresh bread, French toast, yogurt, and a wide variety of fruit. We left Niagara-on-the-Lake to return to Tiago's house in Toronto and awaiting us back home was my Canadian immigration paperwork.

Tiago and I planned to complete the sponsorship application together; we decided it would be best for us to get married first. The sponsorship application listed a ton of questions and required proof that Tiago and I were committed in our relationship. They requested that I provide letters, gifts, and photos. They specifically wanted us to quantify how much money we spent on these gifts, and they wanted us to share photos that Tiago and I took with friends and families from both sides. We had already started the application process. We selected our wedding date to take place during mid-December of 2002, one month away.

We were so excited to announce our exciting news to everyone, but we planned our wedding on such short notice that we knew that our parents and some of our closest friends would not to be able to attend. We decided to have a formal celebration later, when everyone could share our special day with us. As I was about to share the news with my mother over the phone, Tiago asked for her blessing to marry me. She was overjoyed by his proposal and gave him her blessing to marry me.

On a rainy mid-December morning, Tiago and I prepared to celebrate our wedding day. I wanted it to be intimate and peaceful, the most beautiful day of my life. The ceremony was conducted in English, and even though the language was not as familiar to me, we all got emotional from the reverend's beautiful words.

As I stood before the reverend looking deep into Tiago's eyes, I could see the laughs, the tears of joy, the dates, and the stories we shared reflected into my soul. I could see a vision of our future together, growing old with this devoted man and starting a family together. The room filled with love and grace as the reverend concluded the beautiful ceremony. When we left city hall, a colourful rainbow appeared across the sky, and I knew that we were being blessed from above with a promised future.

We celebrated our honeymoon and New Year's Eve in Niagara Falls. Winter in Canada is harsh; I had never experienced temperatures quite like it before. I wasn't used to wearing a down-filled coat, a toque, and snow boots to survive the simple act of stepping foot outside our front door. Growing up in Chambéry, I was used to seeing only a dusting of snow. It was usually the mountains that had heavy snowfalls. Here in Canada, it felt like an endless blizzard of snow blanketing the streets every time I stepped out. The days were short, the nights were long, and I felt as though the sun had abandoned me. There were many gloomy days where all I saw outside were bright grey clouds. I preferred to stay at home and hibernate. I felt like I was being threatened by the harsh Canadian winters even as the days grew closer to spring. The more I lived through the cold climate, the more I longed to return to Portugal.

I wanted to regain a sense of independence for myself. I didn't have an Ontario driver's license. Don't get me wrong, I loved going out with Tiago to the grocery store or to run errands with him, but I knew I needed to start driving again. For some reason, Ontario would allow me to drive as a tourist, but after an extended period I had to complete a driver's license test in Ontario. It was almost as if nothing I brought to Canada was acceptable, not even my Portuguese license. Everything had to be renewed.

Even though I was married to a Canadian citizen I was not legal yet, meaning I was not eligible for health coverage. Any social services that I needed, including healthcare, had to be paid in full. I worried about getting sick while my sponsorship application was being processed, because I did not want to put Tiago in a position where he would have to pay for my healthcare and medicine.

By the end of 2003, one year into my marriage with Tiago, my sponsorship application was denied. We decided to hire an experienced immigration lawyer to help us. My lawyer had been an immigration official for several years, and he knew the sponsorship process and the immigration laws like the back of his hand. For the second time, I completed a sponsorship application with the lawyer. Once again, I had to provide X-rays, health tests, and a police background check on top of the letters, pictures, and marriage certificate that I had provided in my previous application. He was an amazing lawyer, but we spent an overwhelming amount of money in our attempts to change my status to a permanent resident.

The process made me feel discouraged. I wanted to leave. I disliked the country, the language, and the cold. The winter was very hard; sometimes the sun would not appear for days. These gloomy weeks were very difficult. I couldn't even go back to Portugal without fear of being denied at the Canadian border. I felt like a prisoner locked in a country where I hadn't committed any crime. I felt punished for falling in love with a Canadian.

Spring of 2004 had arrived, and on the day of my champagne birthday—the date was the same as the age I was turning—I received a letter from Immigration Canada inviting me to leave the country. Initially, I was terrified and completely desperate. They wanted me to return to Portugal and wait for the results of my sponsorship application. How could this be? Tiago and I were married; how could they expect me to wait in Portugal while my husband was in Canada?

I immediately called the lawyer, and he thankfully assured me that the letter hadn't specified a date, so there was still hope. The letter didn't mention that I would be deported, it just mentioned that I was invited to leave. My lawyer said I could stay in Canada unless I received another letter with a specified date. The whole process had devastated me. I felt like this fucking system was failing me. We had spent so much money on my legalization, money that we could have used to renovate or buy a bigger home.

It had been almost two years since I had moved to Canada. I understood English a lot better than before but speaking it was still challenging. I did not feel comfortable talking to people around me without feeling self-conscious. When Tiago and I went out in group settings, I had a hard time expressing myself without fear of people commenting on my heavy French accent, or on the way that I pronounced certain words. We could be around friends and family who jokingly picked on my speech and understood Portuguese, but God forbid they tried speaking Portuguese, because they didn't want to ridicule themselves. They did not understand that it made me feel more uncomfortable with the language, and it was taking a toll on my self-esteem. Canada is a bilingual nation, yet in many circumstances I felt like an outsider in Toronto whenever I tried to express myself in French. It seemed like nobody in Toronto spoke the French language fluently. It was a never-winning battle to try to assimilate into groups that wouldn't welcome my French or my poor English.

With the arrival of June, Catarina and Beatriz came to visit me for a week. I was thrilled to see them, and I could not wait for them to meet Tiago. When I picked them up from the airport, we were overjoyed to see each other. I had missed them tremendously, and it was as though I had never left Portugal when I reunited with them. They fell in love with Tiago immediately. Both Catarina and Beatriz were only children. In just a few hours, Tiago became like a big brother to them.

It was so special to see the love of my life with my best friends. Their interactions flowed beautifully. Catarina started joking around with Tiago. She was sharp with her English. She understood the nuances of the English language much better than I did. It was hilarious to see her interact with Tiago, while Beatriz and I would sit back and try to figure out what they were talking about.

The week of their visit flew so quickly. For many months I felt like I was losing a part of myself every day. I felt invisible at times. After months of feeling discouraged and homesick, their visit reignited a spark in me. I needed to feel their love, and their stay reminded me of who I was before I left Portugal. It was the first time I felt like the Émilie I had left behind in Portugal had finally been brought back to life.

Three months passed, and the changing colours of the September leaves welcomed me with some surprising news. I woke up one morning and realized that I was a few days late in my menstrual cycle. And suddenly, the smell of coffee made me nauseated.

"You're pregnant. You look pregnant," Anais said to me.

"Don't joke. There's no way. We've been careful," I said.

"There is a glow in your face. I can see it. I'm going to be an auntie!"

I didn't think this was possible. I only wanted to get pregnant after my legalization. I completed four different pregnancy tests on the same day at my sister's house, but each test confirmed that, I was positive.

"These could be false positives. I need to go to the doctor," I said.

"The doctor is going to tell you what I already know," she said, giggling.

I went to the doctor's office the following day. I completed a urine sample, and within minutes the doctor confirmed that I was pregnant. Tiago was over the moon: he was going to be a father. Anais was beyond happy. I called my mother and she cried with tears of joy. Her baby girl was going to be a mommy.

During my pregnancy, I tried to access local community centres to see if there were doctors that would be willing to see me at a lower cost, but the doors were closed on me once again. Every blood test, every ultrasound, every routine checkup required me to pay everything out of pocket because I was not a permanent resident or a Canadian citizen yet. Then I had the blessing of meeting a wonderful obstetrician who accommodated an affordable price for me. He too was outraged that Tiago, a Canadian citizen, had to pay for his wife's medical bills out of pocket while many people who entered the country were covered by government subsidies. It felt unfair.

When my lawyer found out that I was pregnant, he issued a letter to Immigration Canada, begging them to process my application faster since I was soon to give birth to a Canadian citizen.

During my pregnancy, I decided to focus on improving my English. I was going to be a mother, and I knew I would have to advocate for myself and my child. I started reading books in English with a French-English dictionary next to me. I started watching English Channels with English subtitles to help improve my literacy. I was committed to learning the language, and I would practice my English with Tiago when he returned home from work.

By the time I was eight months pregnant, Tiago was working long hours to make more money for our family. We were hoping I would have a smooth delivery, but we also factored in that complications could occur during my delivery. The hospital told us that if I needed a caesarean section, it would cost us over $10,000. Knowing how expensive the delivery could be brought me a tremendous amount of stress. I was already nervous about giving birth to a child, and the thought of having complications terrified me.

My mother flew to Toronto to be with me a week before my delivery. By April 2005, I gave birth to a beautiful healthy boy named David. Becoming a mother felt like my heart was coming out of my chest, and before I knew it, I was holding a beautiful angel in my arms. God gifted me this child, and I promised to guide this angel with my life. I looked at this little baby and I felt a huge sense of joy. I gazed at him while he was sleeping in my arms, and I knew that I loved this child more than I could express. I promised to protect him and love him forever.

The voice of self-doubt echoed in me as I held David in my arms. I kept wondering: Will I be enough for him? Will I be strong enough to give everything my child needed? Am I going to be a good mom? I was so scared of the idea of failing him. I needed to make sure that I gave this child everything I never had. I was committed to learning and being the best mother that I could be, but at what point would I know whether I was giving him enough?

A month after David's birth, I received my visa, which gave me permanent residency status in Canada. Finally, I no longer had to live with an illegal status, and I could raise a family in peace.

# XV

## MIRRORING THE PAST

Raising David in the first three months was more challenging than I expected. For three months straight David slept very little, day or night. He was severely colicky, so he always appeared uncomfortable, and his pain echoed across the house from his intense crying. To top it off, he would get acid reflux after he ate. It wasn't until August when we finally started feeding him solids and David's pain seemed to simmer down. The acid reflux and the intense crying eventually went away.

At the end of December 2005, when David was eight months old, a heavy winter storm hit us. Tiago had invited his co-worker over for dinner to exchange Christmas gifts and to celebrate the end of the holidays. Throughout the day, as I was preparing for our evening soirée, I felt a painful ache intensify at the joint of my shoulder. I ignored it for most of the evening until I felt a sharp pain shoot across my right arm. It started from my shoulder, travelling down my elbow to my hand. For the entire dinner the pain showed on my face, but I had kept it to myself.

After our guests left, I took some painkillers in hopes that I would feel better. Tiago massaged my arm, thinking that perhaps it was muscle pain that needed to be eased. When he went to bed, I couldn't even lie down next to him because I was in so much pain. It felt as though the painkillers hadn't taken any effect. For the entire night I sat in the corner of my bedroom watching the snow fall as I held my shoulder with my left hand, rocking myself back and forth.

A couple of hours into the early morning, I woke up Tiago because the pain burning in my shoulder was unbearable. He called his mother to watch over David so he could take me to the emergency room.

As soon as his mother arrived, Tiago and I rushed to emergency. The doctors took a blood test and an X-ray to determine if I had any fractures, pinched nerves, or any other irregularities. They narrowed it down to an inflammation that required further testing from a rheumatologist. I wasn't able to raise my elbow past my breast. They could see from my expression that I was suffering, so they gave me two strong pills and had me wait a few hours to see if the pain would subside, but it didn't. As a last resort, they injected my shoulder with cortisone. A few hours passed and the intensity of the pain temporarily subsided.

I had to wait three weeks until my appointment with the rheumatologist. When I went to see him, he gave me a requisition form for a blood screening. I did the tests that he had arranged, and after a few weeks of waiting the doctor confirmed what I was afraid of: rheumatoid arthritis. I knew what this disease was; my mother had suffered for years with rheumatoid polyarthritis. I knew what was going on inside of me. My immune system wasn't recognizing my healthy cells anymore and was attacking them now. There was an inner battlefield going on beyond my understanding.

Why was this happening to me? I had just given birth to my son nine months ago. I'd just became a permanent resident of Canada. My life was supposed to get better from there. But this pain was so severe. At times I couldn't even hold my baby boy. I couldn't open his baby bottle, couldn't hold the spoon up to feed him, couldn't even clip my own bra—Tiago had to help me. I looked at the vanity mirror in my bathroom and saw a reflection of my mother's pain take shape in her youngest daughter's face. She was right: Just like her, I was born to suffer. This was my destiny.

The rheumatologist prescribed a heavy drug meant to suppress my immune system and reduce the painful reactions to my body attacking itself. This medication was a chemotherapy drug, so I was experiencing severe side effects from the medication. Between the hair loss, nausea, diarrhea, and constant fatigue, there were days when I could not find the strength to run between the washroom and my son crying for his mother's love.

On top of this horrible medication, the rheumatologist prescribed me a nonsteroidal anti-inflammatory drug intended to decrease my inflammation and reduce my pain. How were these medications supposed to help me? My body was still suffering from the inflammation, and now I was living with debilitating side effects.

Even though I was living with pain, I put Tiago and David's needs before mine. Like my mother, I worked to clean my house from top to bottom. I did the laundry, I ironed everyone's clothes to perfection, I cooked healthy meals from scratch to feed my family, and I worked with Lily on occasion to help with the bills. But then there were those days, the crisis days, when I just couldn't do it. I felt guilty. My mother was able to handle the upkeep of the house, work in the cleaning industry, and cook for the family despite her condition. I wanted to replicate her devotion, but I couldn't match her abilities. I felt like I was failing my family.

June of 2006 rolled around, and spring finally came. I was five months into my diagnosis, and I felt another sharp pain shoot through on my left hand, and down on my right arm again. The pain was so unbearable that it was impossible to hold back tears.

David had been taking a nap upstairs, so when I heard him wake up, I knew I had to pick him up. Tiago was working an hour away from town, so I called my sister to come over because I knew I wouldn't be able to pick him up from the crib. I mustered the energy to walk up the stairs and be there for my son.

"*Mama! Mama!*" he cried from his crib.

"Mommy is coming, my love," I shouted from the steps.

When I entered his bedroom, David extended his arms with joy. He was ready for me to pick him up, but my arms didn't have the strength, I was in so much pain.

"Mama! Mama!" he shouted.

"Mommy is here. Mommy cannot take you out of the crib because Mommy has boo-boos. But Auntie Anais is coming to get you," I said.

He started getting anxious, throwing his arms up at me and waiting for me to pick him up. He started crying. I wanted to hold my child, but I could not. I kissed his small arms between the bars of the crib. It upset me to see my baby upset.

I couldn't live like this anymore, not at twenty-eight years old. Apparently, there is no cure for rheumatoid arthritis, but I could not live with thinning hair, the constant nausea and diarrhea, on top of the inflammation that I was still feeling in my joints. I needed to make a decision for my life because this pain was debilitating. I couldn't even pick up my own son. I was not living a normal life anymore. What was I doing?

I always tried to think outside the box. It started when I came across Agatha Christie's books, followed by learning about Mother Teresa and Nelson Mandela. At nine years old, these figures were my idols, and since then I had become interested in alternative viewpoints, divergent thinking, and, of course, medical alternatives. My inner voice was telling me to pay attention, to shift my perception of this pain and explore how my mind was influencing it.

Nelson Mandela had always believed in the power of the mind. I started reading *You Can Heal Your Body* by Louise Hay, an author who challenged societal norms in the late '70s, who discussed the connection between the mind and the body. Louise Hay was physically and sexually abused until she moved out of her home at fifteen years old. Later in life, she was diagnosed with cervical cancer.

She was not surprised that her cancer appeared in the region of her body where she was abused. She believed in the metaphysical causes of physical illnesses. By practicing psychotherapy, visualizations, positive self-affirmations, and healthy nutrition, Louise Hay cured herself from her own cancer after six months of her diagnosis.

Her work resonated deeply with me, and it allowed me to reflect on my own circumstances. I believed that my physical pain was directly connected to my emotional pain and my core beliefs. I found a video clip of Deepak Chopra, who was making a guest appearance on *The Oprah Winfrey Show*. Deepak said to Oprah that "every cell in our body is eavesdropping on our internal dialogue, and by changing your internal dialogue, you can influence the chemistry—the fundamental chemistry—of every cell."

I thought to myself, *if our inner dialogue is positive, then by this train of thought, the cells of the body should be functioning normally and harmoniously. But if our inner dialogue is negative, then the messages coming from the mind would, in effect, harm the body, creating an inner battlefield.*

I knew I was battling with many negative emotions that I carried from the bleeding wounds of my childhood. My father was manipulative and controlling, he was emotionally and physically abusive, and he ripped out my self-esteem and my self-worth at a very young age. My mother battled deep depression, she was stuck in the past, and she harboured anger and resentment after my father abandoned us. I knew that reflecting on my childhood was where I needed to start in my healing journey.

I continued the rheumatologist's drug treatment for another few months, but I couldn't endure the side effects anymore, so I made a choice to stop taking all the medication. I needed to learn how my body was inflamed. I started visiting a naturopathic doctor. Soon I learned to look for patterns in my body's reaction to stress and to its reaction to the foods I ate. I noticed that particularly stressful days were often succeeded by a series of sleepless nights and rheumatoid arthritis flareups.

With certain foods, I soon learned how my body reacted to them. For example, if my joints flared shortly after I ate a tomato or a potato, then I would shift my cooking toward making different meals that were friendlier to my body. Eventually, I realized just how important a role nutrition would play on my healing journey.

In looking at ways to care for myself, I visited a spiritual teacher named Jeanie, who opened my world up to self-love, self-care, and meditation. Self-love and self-care were completely foreign concepts to me. Portuguese-raised, I was culturally conditioned to believe that the hierarchy of needs for a Portuguese mother was that the kids were a priority first, then the husband, and then the house. My mother drilled into me that, "The way your children and your husband dress is a direct reflection of who you are as a mother and as a wife." I believed that thinking of me was selfish; I needed to put anyone else's needs before mine. I was certainly at the bottom of the hierarchy. Jeanie and Louise Hay helped me realize how important it is to elevate myself on that hierarchy and how important it is to cultivate self-love.

Since I took myself off the medication, I was no longer suffering from their side effects, but I still had the occasional crisis days. I went to visit my rheumatologist during the summer of 2007, and I told him that I stopped taking the medication he prescribed. He offered to administer cortisone shots every two weeks. I politely declined and refused this treatment too.

"So now you're playing doctor? I am giving you options here, Émilie. You have rheumatoid arthritis. You need to take medication. You can't leave here without this," the doctor snapped.

"I understand. Being my rheumatologist, you are trying to offer me the resources that you have. I tried the medication, but I am still living in pain. The side effects of the medication were not helping me either. This isn't working for me. I want to try something else," I said.

"I am putting you in remission then. By your fortieth birthday, you will be in a wheelchair if you do not take any medication. I can assure you that you will suffer severe degeneration."

"I'll take my chance, doctor."

A couple of months later, the changing leaves of the autumn months rolled around the corner, and Anais and her family decided to move away. Since I had moved to Canada, we had reconnected and become closer, but she and Enzo had decided they wanted to raise their family in France.

At this point, it had been several months since I stopped the medication. Right before the Thanksgiving long weekend, I received a strong sign from the universe. The pharmacy called and Tiago picked up the phone. The pharmacy shared that the anti-inflammatory had been taken off the market for causing liver failure and other serious side effects.

"Oh my god, is this a sign?" Tiago exclaimed, looking at me in disbelief.

"Yes! This is my sign," I said. "This is confirming the path that I've taken."

Three years passed since I had chosen a natural approach in my healing and Anais moved to France. The crisis days would still come and go, but I felt better and lighter about my life overall. To the surprise of my family doctor and my family, I was improving.

My Aunt Aurora, my father's older sister who lived in France, called me during another Canadian winter storm. She explained that my father had remarried to a younger woman and had moved back to Chambéry. He was living in a building across the street from her, and she shared that my father appeared terminally ill with a mysterious illness. He did not know how much longer he had left to live, but he had expressed to my aunt that he didn't want to die without seeking forgiveness and seeing his daughter one last time.

The phone call with my aunt made me feel extremely skeptical. My son was five years old. He had no idea about his grandfather or who he was, and I wasn't sure if I could trust the idea of introducing him to my father. I had been burned in every instance I thought I could trust my father. Everything that came out of his mouth was a lie. Every time I deposited my trust in him, he would hurt me again and again and again. The little Émilie inside of me wanted to reconnect with him to make peace. Perhaps my father re-entering my life was the missing puzzle piece I needed to advance in my healing journey.

After sharing the news about my father with Tiago, we decided that we would go to Portugal in the spring for our birthdays. We planned to fly to Chambéry from Lisbon for two days only at the end of our trip. For me, part of my healing was to be able to forgive my father. I needed to let go of the past so I could finally heal my wounds.

My family and I flew to Portugal first, where we visited the beautiful coastal beaches and my dear friends. David loved spending time with Ana Julia, Ines, Beatriz, Catarina, Alexandro, and Bruna. He referred to all my girlfriends as his "aunties," and everyone played with his chubby cheeks and loved him as their own child.

Once we flew to Chambéry, my family and I stayed with Aunt Aurora. Anais, her kids, and my mother also joined us at my aunt's. The last time I saw my aunt and her sons was fifteen years prior, so there was a lot of hugging, kissing, and catching up to do between our families. My Aunt Aurora was over the moon to see me. She hugged me tightly and welcomed my boys with a warm heart. It was sweet to be in her apartment. I did not have many memories of her family as a child because my father did not allow us to spend much time with them but seeing them took me back to when I was a kid. I was more excited to see my aunt, my cousins, and my family than I was to see my own father.

When the time came to visit my father, my mother stayed behind. As my Aunt Aurora led us across the street toward my father's building, my hands were sweaty, and I felt cold sweats slide down my neck. I hadn't seen my father in several years and I was apprehensive. He was going to meet Tiago and his grandson for the first time. We approached the door of his apartment and Aunt Aurora knocked on the door. When my father opened it, I saw the heavy curve of old age taking form in his arched spine. He had been diagnosed with Parkinson's disease, and I could see the tremors taking a toll on his movement.

He cried when he saw us. He opened his arms to hug me. Looking at him took me to many places, but my body was numb. I couldn't hug him. I kissed him and gently caressed his back instead. Tiago shook his hand. David was a bit hesitant at his greeting, but he ended up giving him a small hug. My father's new wife was from Eastern Europe; she seemed nice, but it was hard to get a real impression of her from such a short visit.

After all those years, I was anticipating an apology or accountability to acknowledge what he had done to me. For someone who expressed how much he wanted to see his daughter before he died, he didn't appear terminally ill, and he didn't seem interested in acknowledging his mistakes either. I was ready to forgive him, but it seemed he wasn't willing to take responsibility for the actions of his past. He didn't want to revisit the past, but I did. I needed closure. I needed answers. I needed more from him.

The following day, we said our goodbyes to Aunt Aurora, my cousins, Anais, and my mother. I found out that my mother needed to run some health tests. She had lost some weight and appeared more tired and weaker than usual. Over the previous five years, my mother had visited us in Canada for long periods, and we visited her each summer in Portugal. She had established a beautiful bond with David. It was through David that I had the privilege of experiencing another side of my mother. She played with him, took him to the park, taught him Portuguese, cooked meals with him, and was fully present with him, which was a bonding experience that I never shared with my mother. Saying goodbye to his grandmother was heartbreaking for him.

Three months passed since we saw my mother, and by July 2010, my life changed forever. I was in the middle of preparing breakfast for my family and made my routine morning phone call to my mother. When she picked up the phone, I knew immediately that something was wrong. She shared that her rheumatologist had her stay in the clinic to run some more health tests. She took a deep breath and shared her news.

"My daughter . . . *t*hey found cancer on my lung and . . . it does not look good. I am going to die."

# XVI

## THE MALIGNANT REAPPEARANCE

My mother's words struck me like lightning. I thought I was going to pass out. I took a deep breath and tried to regain control of myself. I struggled to accept her words. I thought I must have misunderstood, but suddenly our worlds were turned upside down.

"Maman . . . Maman, what are you talking about?" I said while fighting tears back and trying to remain calm.

"With all the testing I have been doing, my rheumatologist found two tumours on my lung, and there is no way to remove them. I have lung cancer, *Émilie,*" my mother restated, starting to cry.

"Maman, you are going to be okay. Y–you are the strongest woman I know. I must call your doctor . . . I need to understand what is going on. You need to run all the tests before jumping to conclusions. I am here, I will be here for you," I reassured her.

"Oh *Émilie,* I wish you were here. You are so far away. Your sister has her own family and her own life here. I can't expect her to take care of me. I am going to die. My mother died at sixty-two years old, I am sixty-nine. It is my turn," my mother lamented.

"I promise I will speak to Anais. We will have all of this sorted out. Don't worry, Maman."

I texted my sister immediately and told her we needed to talk. How could I help my mother? I was so far away; I needed to be with her. She was suffering by herself. I felt powerless being across the ocean, away from her.

Since my sister had moved back to Chambéry, her life had been challenging. She withdrew from us and was living completely in her head. She was not fully present with my mother, but I hoped the diagnosis would bring her back to reality.

The following morning at three a.m., I woke up to call my mother's rheumatologist in Chambéry to gain a deeper understanding of my mother's diagnosis. It was nine a.m. in France when I called Dr. Bou, who explained that she had two tumours on opposite extremities of the same lung. One of the tumours was bleeding, so it was too dangerous to perform what's called a transthoracic needle biopsy.

The rheumatologist knew that the cancer was malignant, but he needed the tissue to understand the nature of the cancer and what stage it was at. I was fearful—the fact that surgery was not an option reduced her chance of remission. I did my best not to think about it too much, otherwise it would have worried me to death. Dr. Bou was going to keep my mother in the clinic for further testing and would be in contact with me to update me on the results.

Once Tiago woke up, I told him I needed to be an advocate for my mother's health. Since it was summer, many healthcare workers in France were on vacation. I knew my mother needed me. And I knew that if I travelled to France to be with her, I could ask the professionals the right questions and push for more answers.

My concern was that my mother lived on the fourth floor of a building without an elevator. She had been on a waiting list for admission to a retirement home for almost a year without success. If she were to undergo treatments that would impact her breathing and make her weak, then how would she be able to walk up four flights of stairs?

I always saw my mother as invincible. Since I was a little girl, I always saw my mother as a superwoman. Even though she lived with depression, my father left us, and she had to rebuild from ashes. This woman moved mountains; her will and strength were incredible.

As a child I never feared my death, but I was petrified at the idea of losing someone close to me. I felt anxious and scared and wasn't sure how I would be able to survive the pain.

Wanting to be there for my mother, I made the decision to leave for France for six weeks to help her when she needed me the most. Tiago and I decided that David would come with me since Tiago would be working, and it would be too long for David to be away from me. Coming from a household where my parents were never open with us, I promised myself to be as transparent and open with my children as I could be throughout their lives.

There would be times during my trip to France where I would have to leave David with my Aunt Aurora to accompany my mother to her doctor's appointments. My son deserved an explanation beforehand, but I was worried about being honest with him about his grandmother's health.

I decided to speak with David's paediatrician to figure out the best approach to communicate this situation to my five-year-old. The paediatrician recommended not to give him an extensive amount of information. She advised me that I should explain to David that his grandmother was not feeling well, and that she would be having a lot of tests done and seeing a lot of doctors. If he had any questions, I should answer them as simply as possible.

After speaking with the paediatrician, Tiago and I sat down with David and explained that his *vovó*—"grandmother" in Portuguese, was sick and we needed to help her in France. I told him that he would come with me to visit his grandmother, and he was delighted. Thankfully, he did not ask any questions about her health and seemed excited to visit her again. He was going to miss his daddy, but we promised to call him every day.

A few days before I left for France at the end of July, I fell under the weather with a sinus infection and my rheumatoid arthritis crept up on me. My head was hurting, and I had slept poorly during the nights leading up to our departure. I was haunted by the suffering that lay ahead for my mother. Since surgery was not possible for her because the cancer was on polarizing ends of her lung, she would have to do chemotherapy and radiation therapy. I was scared that the treatment would destroy her. Her immune system was already weak from rheumatoid polyarthritis.

Ever since I had seen my father a few months back, we would phone in every now and then. When he heard from my Aunt Aurora that my mother was diagnosed with cancer, he tried to be supportive. He insisted that I should stay with him when I visited France, but I wasn't open to his idea. I wasn't comfortable with him. It just didn't seem like a good idea to mix the stress of my mother's health with his sudden reappearance, knowing that he had been absent for several years. After I expressed that I would be staying with Aunt Aurora, he was not too pleased, but he didn't argue.

We flew to France and arrived on a Thursday morning. My mother's first appointment was the following morning with Dr. Bou. When I arrived at my mother's apartment, she appeared different from when I had last seen her. She had become visibly frail. She had lost more weight, her eyes appeared very small, she had collarbone ganglions circling her neck, and she had dark shadows embedded around her eyes. I could see the fear in them. She hugged me and David as soon as she opened her door to welcome us.

"Vovó, don't worry. We are here to take care of you; you will be fine. Right, Mommy?" David said, looking at me happily with his sweet hazel eyes.

"Right, my love. Vovó is going to be just fine," I reassured him. She needed to be fine. *I* needed her to be fine.

My mother's apartment was a five-minute walk from my Aunt Aurora's. It was a small studio with a tiny kitchenette and a couch that wasn't big enough for the three of us, which is why we stayed with my aunt.

The following morning, I woke up to my aunt unravelling fresh bread and croissants that she had picked up from the bakery. I had no appetite because I was worried about my mother's appointment that day, but it was a thoughtful gesture to wake up to. She was going to stay with David for a couple of hours so I could accompany my mother to her appointment.

When it was time to leave, I went to pick my mother up from her apartment and found her waiting outside of her building door. I gave her a kiss and put my arm around her as we walked silently side by side to her appointment.

We arrived at the rheumatologist's office, where he greeted us, and he was delighted I had accompanied my mom for support. My mother had been Dr. Bou's patient for almost fifteen years.

"So, Maria, on Monday you will have the transthoracic needle biopsy at ten a.m. at the hospital," Dr. Bou said. His voice was short.

I was confused. For the last several weeks when I spoke with him over the phone, he had reiterated that the transthoracic needle biopsy was too dangerous because one of her tumours was bleeding. It had to be very precise, with no margin for error.

"What do you mean, Dr. Bou? I thought you said she cannot do this procedure. You said it yourself: it's too dangerous! How could you be sending her to a biopsy appointment on Monday?"

"We need to know the nature of the cancer. We need to start this treatment as soon as possible. We cannot wait any longer; it is what it is. Your mom has to do it," he responded with an irritated tone.

"Says who, Dr. Bou? Aren't you contradicting yourself? For the last two weeks, you have been telling us that this particular biopsy cannot be done on my mom's tumour because it could be fatal. Now, suddenly, you are saying that this procedure is, okay?" There was a moment of silence, and then I said, "Absolutely not. Take the phone and cancel her appointment. I don't approve of this decision. Let's find a safer way to do a biopsy." He straightened his body on the chair and looked at me furiously.

"Excuse me? Who is the doctor here? What are you doing, Émilie? Did you come here to kill your mother? She must present herself on Monday to do the biopsy. She must do it. There is no question," he asserted. I stood up from the chair and glared at him, livid.

"No, Dr. Bou! On the contrary, I came to *save* my mother from *you*. Who are you, Dr. Bou? A rheumatologist. Are we talking about arthritis? No, we are talking about cancer. From this point forward, I will not be dealing with you, I will be talking with the pulmonologist. We are done here. This conversation is over," I said.

I assisted my poor mother up from the chair. She was shaken and in disbelief. Her tiny eyes appeared like a lost child's. My mother had always been obedient when it came to doctors' orders. I knew my mother did not want to go against these, but in this case, I felt Dr. Bou was wrong. How could a doctor contradict himself after telling his patient confidently that the procedure was dangerous? I needed to advocate for her.

On our way down the stairs, she began to break down in tears.

"Maman, don't worry, everything will be okay. I promise to take care of you. I need to advocate for you, Maman. Trust me! You cannot do this procedure. We are going to find another way. The pulmonologist is the right doctor to help you. Dr. Bou is out of his league. This is no longer rheumatology," I reassured her.

My stomach turned upside down when we left the clinic. I was angry and hurt. How could he say I came here to kill my mother? Who dares to say that to a daughter looking after their mother? My heart ached for my dear mother. She already had to deal with the cancer diagnosis, and now she had to deal with unnecessary complications?

We returned to my aunt's house, though my mother appeared so sad. When she saw David, her world lit up again. He gave her a hug as soon as she walked through the door. He was so happy to see her. Aunt Aurora invited her to stay for lunch. We decided that after eating, I would treat my family to an ice cream, take David on a stroll down memory lane, and bring him to the playground next to the elementary school I attended in Chambéry.

When we came back from our after-lunch stroll, my mother seemed much calmer. I booked an appointment with her pulmonologist for Monday. I called Anais and insisted she join us. We needed to shower my mother with support, and we needed to be together again.

Every evening, my father invited me and David over for dinner. We usually accepted his dinner invitations, but I made sure to cut them short because I was tired and emotionally drained. He kept insisting that we stay with him for the night, but I declined because I was already comfortable with my aunt.

On Sunday evening, the evening before Anais and I accompanied my mother to the pulmonologist appointment, I had dinner at my father's. I was trying to seek some compassion from him. I explained the recent doctor's visit, and he looked at me with a calm, almost condescending expression.

"You know Émilie, it is life. You need to mentalize that your mother is going to die," he said naturally, with a hint of joy in his tone. His words reignited emotions from my past.

"She is not going to die, and I have nothing to mentalize myself about. I don't appreciate this comment. It is not helpful, Papa," I quickly retorted. And just like that I was in fight or flight mode, and I felt in danger again.

"I'm sorry, I didn't mean to upset you," he said emotionlessly. He apologized just to say he did it, but I did not feel any sincerity behind his words.

"Émilie, tomorrow I am off work. I am thinking that if you want us to watch over David while you are at the appointment with your mom, we will take him to Chateau de Buisson-Rond for an ice-cream and show him around the park," his wife said to me in French.

I thought about it for a second. I switched to my English tongue and looked at my son.

"David, are you comfortable with staying with your grandfather tomorrow afternoon? He wants to take you to the park."

"Sure, Mama!" he said.

"Thank you. David will stay with you," I said in French.

We returned to my aunt's house. When I went to bed that night, David fell asleep beside me, and I cried myself to sleep. I was not a doctor, but I felt strongly that I had made the right decision for my mother. I couldn't stop thinking about what my father had said. His tone was too suggestive. I sensed a storm approaching. Was he going to help me here? Or was he going to crush me again?

Monday arrived, and I left David with my father while Anais and I accompanied my mother to the pulmonologist's office. We met with the pulmonologist, who was in his late fifties and appeared very pleasant. He examined the tests that my mother took with Dr. Bou, and he knew that I had cancelled the transthoracic needle biopsy.

"Doctor, due to the danger of the biopsy that Dr. Bou warned me about, I was the one who ordered the cancellation of the biopsy. He described the procedure as highly dangerous, and I wasn't keen on allowing my mother to go through with it," I said.

He smiled and looked at my mother.

"You are in good hands, Maria. Your daughter is right. I would have been against this procedure as well. The biopsy would have been far too dangerous in your particular circumstance," he explained.

He went around his desk and sat by my mother.

"Is it okay if I touch the area around your neck?" he asked politely.

"Of course, you can, doctor," my mother humbly replied. He gently felt the ganglions circling her collarbone.

"There it is—she is full of ganglions. We just need to take tissue from them. It will be a small surgery, and it will be completely safe.

Once we have the results, we will know what the best course of treatment will be from here. I will arrange to have you see a specialist for a consultation, who will then perform the small surgery and remove tissue from the ganglions," he said.

My mom looked at me with tears of relief. She knew I was there to protect her and not let anyone hurt her. She was relieved that I had made the right call, and the pulmonologist had confirmed it. I experienced some relief from the pulmonologist's visit, but I was still feeling uneasy. I could not wait to see David, and I had a feeling that I needed to go pick him up. I wasn't used to having my son taken care of by anyone else except for my mother and mother-in-law. Knowing that David was with my father and his wife, whom I didn't know well, I felt I needed to cut his time short with them.

After the appointment, I went back to my father's apartment. As soon as my father opened the door, David ran behind him and jumped in my arms. He hugged me tightly.

"I am so happy to see you, Mama!" he shouted with joy.

My father and his wife invited me to stay over for dinner again, but I declined. We left his apartment, and on our way back to my aunt's apartment, David looked up at me.

"Mommy, I don't want to stay with your father anymore. If I have to stay with someone when you go to the doctor with Vovó, I want to stay with Aunt Aurora," he said to me.

"Did something happen?" I looked at him concerned. "Was he not nice to you? Was his wife not nice to you? Did he do something?"

"No, they were nice, Mommy! They got me a car and an ice cream. I would just rather stay with Aunt Aurora."

Why was *my son* feeling this way? This was not a good thing. Children are more in tune with the energy around them than adults; they *feel* things that don't need words. David must have sensed something from them during his visit.

We returned to my aunt's apartment, and my cousins surprised us with a lovely visit. We had many good laughs, and it brought me so much joy. In my childhood, we never had the chance to create memories with each other. My cousins loved my mother.

Even though my father was Aurora's brother, they respected and cherished my mother more. They did not speak with my father, nor did they trust him. Aunt Aurora made a wonderful dinner, and it was beautiful to be surrounded by my family who loved and supported us during a time when I needed emotional support. Everything that evening felt so natural and effortless.

The next morning, I phoned the hospital to follow up on my mother's small surgery. Since the specialist was going on vacation, all the appointments had been postponed to the end of August or early September. There was nothing that we could do for another few weeks.

My mother said to my aunt in passing that she wished she could return to her hometown in Portugal. I had noticed that she was a passive participant during her own doctor appointments, not participating or questioning anything that the doctors were saying or arranging for her. Nelson Mandela once said, "If you talk to a man in a language he understands, that goes to his head. If you talk to him in his own language, that goes to his heart." What my mother needed right then was to be able to participate in her own health, in her own language. I decided that if there was a time to fulfill my mother's wish to return to Portugal, now was the time to do it.

My friends Catarina and Beatriz were both nurses, so I decided to ask them if they could find a good pulmonologist in Lisbon for a private consultation in August. It was an impulsive decision, and it was challenging during the summer to find an available specialist, but they managed to get a pulmonologist for a private consultation. Once I got the date for our appointment with the specialist, they had found for us, I booked our flights to visit Portugal for two weeks, and my mother was overjoyed.

A couple of days later, I mentioned to my father during dinner that I would be taking my mother to a pulmonologist in Lisbon, and our departure was scheduled for the following evening. My father seemed displeased, but he invited David and me for an early lunch the next day before we had to go to the airport. The timing was inconvenient, but because he and his wife were insistent that we meet with them, I eventually gave in.

Thursday morning rolled around, and our flight was scheduled for seven that night. David and I walked over to my father's apartment. As soon as his wife opened the door, I felt something *off* in the air. I could not pinpoint what it was, but I had an unpleasantly familiar feeling chill my spine as I walked in. We had a surface-level conversation during lunch. His wife cleaned up the dining table, and she offered me a coffee before we left.

David and I sat on the armchair in their living room while my father sat down on the brown leather couch directly across from us. When his wife came with the hot drinks, she sat next to my father and started.

"Émilie, it is so noble what you are doing for your mother. You came here all the way from Canada, and here you are, fighting for her. You are truly amazing, and such a good daughter. Now, remember, you are responsible for your father *as well*. Don't forget that. Are you going to do the same for your father as you are doing for your mother?" his wife asked in French.

"Well, to be honest, there is a difference between my mom and dad. Where my mother has always been by my side and never abandoned me, my father forgot that he was my father and abandoned me at thirteen years old," I replied defensively in French. "Let's just stop right here. This is not a conversation we should be having."

"Your dad is a good dad. It is your responsibility to take care of your father the same way that you are taking care of your mother. You are his daughter."

"As I said before, let's stop this conversation right now," I asserted firmly.

"You don't know what your mother has done to our lives, Émilie. She was the one who kept all the money. She was hiding all the money in pots, and that's why our family went bankrupt. She's responsible for destroying our lives, and now you wonder why she is sick. It is because God is punishing her for her sins," my father said, inserting himself into the conversation with his sick venom.

"All of the brothers and sisters at the congregation love your father. He is a good dad. They all say that it's your mom that is not a good person," she said.

My father reached over next to him to pick up his black leather briefcase. He opened it and pulled out the Bible.

"Papa, are you kidding me? I thought you wanted to reconnect with me to make peace and apologize for your mistakes." I started to raise my voice. "We both know what you did. I lived through it, remember? So please stop. This is the perfect chance for you to support me, like you never did before. I need to feel your love, your care and support, not drama, lies, or confusion."

"Émilie, I am telling the truth. Your mom is a witch," he said confidently. "She is facing God's punishment."

"Enough!" I stood up from the armchair and slammed the table forcefully with my fist. The coffee spilled from the cups. I was mad. My son grabbed my hand.

"In the moment that I need you the most, when I need you to be the father that you never were, here you are, choosing to spread your poison yet again. You are heartless, you are cruel, and you have no compassion! How can you be so filled with lies? I am so ashamed to be related to you. Now, to answer your question," I said, directing my attention to his wife. "Will I move one finger to help my father? No, I will not."

My father stood up from the couch and looked me directly in the eye.

"You . . . you are like your mother, but you are the worst witch," he said to me in a repugnant tone. It was a tone I heard so many times as a child, and it was way too familiar to me.

"Of course, Papa, I am the Devil's child, remember? I am your daughter," I said defiantly, feeling my mind slowly return to its body after nearly denting his table.

I took my son, who had his hand clutched in mine throughout the entire argument and stormed out of his apartment. David had never seen me this furious before. But the good thing was he did not comprehend French, so he had no idea what had been said. I took him to the bottom of the staircase of the building, and I kneeled down to hug him.

"I am so sorry that you had to see Mommy lose her temper. Baby, I apologize. I tried very hard to control myself, but your grandpa was telling hurtful lies, and I lost it," I told him shamefully.

"Mommy, it's okay. Promise me not to see him again. He is not nice to you, Mommy, and I don't think he is a nice grandpa" he said, touching my face with his little hands.

"I promise I will not take you there anymore. I promise, my love. Now, David, let's hurry and get ready to go to Portugal! *Yeehaw!*" I said, wiping a teardrop from my cheek.

Catarina and Beatriz picked us up at the airport in Lisbon. We stayed at Beatriz's apartment for the night. It was refreshing to see them again. Catarina and my mother entertained David while I was in the other room with Beatriz, preparing a bed for my mother.

"Let us help you, Émilie," she said softly to me. "We are here to support you and your mother, and you can count on us!" She hugged me and held me in her arms.

I found it challenging to collect myself and put aside the lunch visit I'd had at my father's. Being in Portugal, close to my dear friends, I received the love and support that I needed during this time. I was searching for it from my father, but my real loved ones were my soul sisters right in front of me.

On the days that Catarina, Beatriz and Ana Julia had off from work, we spent as much time together as we could, going to beaches and parks with David. Right before my mother's consultation with her pulmonologist, I prepared all her medical records and tests for him to see. This pulmonologist had done his medical education in France, so I knew he would be able to interpret my mother's test results since they were written in French.

Catarina and Beatriz stayed to watch David while my mother and I went to her appointment. My mother felt more at ease that she was able to have a fluent conversation in Portuguese with the doctor. He reiterated everything that all the doctors in France shared with her, but she felt more comfortable being able to ask questions about her health on her own.

"Doctor, how long do I have to live?" my mother asked him.

"I cannot tell you how long you have left to live. I am not God, but I can tell you that I see patients and I think to myself that some only have six months left to live, but they show up to my office seven years later. Then I have patients who have a good prognosis, but after six months they die. Unfortunately, I don't have an answer to your question. I can advise you on the treatments and assure that it will give you more time, but I believe that is only 50 percent. From what I have experienced, the other 50 percent of the disease is what is connected with the faith and the will of the patient and God," he replied in a kind tone.

We left the doctor's office and returned to Beatriz's apartment. My mother sat down next to me and held my hand.

"I am going to fight this. I still want to have more time with my little star. I want to see him grow just a little more," she said.

The little star she was referring to was David. We silently cried.

Our two-week trip to Portugal soon came to an end. When we returned to France, I spoke with a social worker to help us accelerate the process for my mother's admission to a retirement home. My mother's health was declining from her cancer, and her apartment was no longer suitable for her condition.

Before I left for Canada, I had a serious talk with Anais and told her she needed to step up and be there for our mother since I couldn't. My mother never abandoned us, and we needed to take care of her. Anais promised she would be there for my mother.

I've always carried a sense of loss since I moved to Canada. I couldn't be physically close to who I wanted to be with, and so many special moments were missed because we were so far away. It was heartbreaking to leave my mother behind. My heart was aching from the guilt of not being able to stay with her. I wished I could take my mother to Canada with me, but the whole immigration process was just too complicated, and she wouldn't be covered under a health plan. I felt powerless.

For the first time in my life, I started to live day by day. I was not able to schedule anything anymore. I started looking at the present in a whole new light because I could no longer project a future that was not promised. I understood I had to value the preciousness of the moment, the gift of the present.

I was so angry at God. I was so angry at the world. Everything was beyond my control. My mother was ill, and she needed me. I felt split in two between my boys in Canada and my beloved mother in France. When was my mother ever going to have a break? I was upset with God, disappointed in Him. Why her? Why not my father? I didn't need him, but I needed my *maman*.

# XVII

## MA PETITE MAMAN

I was back home in Toronto, but my heart was with my mother. With the time difference between France and Canada, I was forced to be awake at all hours of the night, touching base with her and her doctors. I needed to make sure that I knew every step of my mother's cancer treatment. I suffered from insomnia, and I was constantly worried, but I needed to be there for her, despite being overseas.

In the fall of 2010, my mother began her strong round of chemotherapy. Even though we pushed to have my mother admitted to a retirement home, she continued to be waitlisted. In the meantime, her best friend Carolina and my Aunt Aurora made sure she was taken care of. They brought her cooked meals, groceries, and anything else she needed. Our family friend, Madame Minda, invited her to stay at her place while she tried to help my mother find a new apartment. Even her pulmonologist, who knew she lived alone on the fourth floor of a building with no elevator, admitted her to stay overnight at the hospital so she could be taken care of by nurses after her chemotherapy treatments. My mother was known for having a generous heart, and many people looked after her when I couldn't be there.

At times, it felt like my sister was not fully present throughout my mother's treatment. Anais had her moments. She would take my mother to appointments and pick her up, but only on occasion. Occasionally, Anais visited or checked in on my mother, and when she did her visits were short. I felt completely helpless. I wanted to be physically present for my mother, but I couldn't.

There were moments when my body ached, I could not breathe, my chest felt tight, and I was emotionally consumed by sadness and guilt. I called my mother up to five times a day, and David spoke to her during his breakfasts, except when she was in treatment. He and I started drawing pictures and writing letters to France with reminders of how strong she was. Her chemotherapy treatment ran for about six months, until they began radiation treatment by March of 2011. My mother would be turning seventy years old by mid-spring, and it was our plan to celebrate her milestone birthday during our summer trip to Portugal, if the doctors approved. I could not wait to be held by my mother's arms again and reconnect with our closest friends and family.

When July arrived, my family and I travelled to Algarve in the southernmost region of Portugal, known for its Atlantic beaches and golf resorts. We were finally going to see my mother, almost a year after our last visit. My mother fought with all her might through her treatments. And while we knew that remission was only a miracle, the doctor had given her the green light to travel.

When we finally saw my mother, she looked beautiful. Her hair was healthy, and her skin was smooth and natural. Most chemotherapy treatments result in hair loss, but thankfully for my mother, she did not lose any of her already thin hair. She suffered from other side effects, but she stood strong overall.

For the first week of our visit, she appeared well. David was over the moon to see her, and we spent our time out and about together. My mother shared that she had a little bit of pain in her hip, but it was a familiar pain for her, and we thought that perhaps it was her rheumatoid polyarthritis acting up.

Even though she was diligent with her medication, the pain intensified within a week to the point where she had difficulty walking. Getting up from bed or walking a few steps felt like running a marathon to her. She would be completely drenched in sweat whenever she tried. Concerned, I contacted her pulmonologist in

France, who advised us to shorten her stay and go back to France. We tried to massage her hip and assist her in other ways, which gave her some temporary relief.

We travelled to Lisbon two weeks after staying in Algarve. We threw a beautiful birthday celebration for my mother in Lisbon, with her friends, family, and people close to our hearts all around us, witnessing this magnificent woman turn seventy years old.

By the time September arrived, my family had already left for Toronto and my mother returned to France. The pulmonologist took her in immediately upon her return to run more tests because she could hardly move.

A couple of weeks passed, and my sister called and shared my mother's devastating test results. My mother's cancer had metastasized to her bones, which explained why she was in so much pain during our summer visit. My knees hit the ground, the world around me started spinning, and every inch of my body echoed with pain. Her cancer was spreading, and I felt like I was going to lose her. I had feared these words for so long. I did not want to believe what was being said. I wanted to have faith that we were going to find a solution. My mother was a fighter, and she was going to fight this cancer.

"God, why are you not protecting her?" I bellowed with tears, "Why my maman? Why must she suffer? Please God, I won't ask for anything else, but please don't take her away from me."

After two years of waiting, my mother was finally admitted to a retirement home in December. David and I flew to Europe on New Year's Day of 2012 to visit her in Chambéry. We were going to stay in a guest apartment on the floor above my mother at the retirement home. Right before we visited, Anais mentioned that my mother did not appear well.

When we saw my mother, she was lying in her bed. She started crying the moment she saw us. Since I had last seen her, her cheeks had caved in, her skin had yellowed, and she had lost more weight. David ran up to her bed to hug and kiss her. However, her appearance and her weak condition worried me, so I decided to phone the pulmonologist, who recommended bringing her to the hospital. My mother did not want to go because David and I were there, but it was necessary—we learned later that she was dehydrated.

During my mother's stay at the hospital, the pulmonologist wrote a requisition for a hospital bed to be placed in her apartment for comfort. My mother needed to take supplements because she was not eating and was low on nutrients. Knowing that I would be taking care of her, the doctor released her within a few days and gave us recommendations for the next level of care.

Once we returned to her apartment, I made my mother feel comfortable in her room and assisted her with anything she needed. When I sat by her bedside, she looked at me warm-heartedly.

"Émilie, my beautiful daughter, I can die peacefully at home. I don't want to die in the hospital," my mother said softly.

"Maman," I said, holding her hand and gently rocking it, "I will do my best to honour your wish. But if I believe that your condition is causing you to suffer and feel that you need some help or assistance, I may need to take you to the hospital so they can look after you and take care of you. I want what is best for you, Maman."

In the time I spent with my mother, many of my friends and family came to visit us. Our close family friend Sabrina, who was Tina and Valerio's oldest daughter, loved my mother like an aunt and invited us to her house. When my mother asked for soup during her visit, Sabrina happily prepared her a bowl and my mother devoured it with enormous satisfaction. It was wonderful to create memories with all the people we loved. Who knew something as simple as soup made with love would bring my mother and me so much joy?

David knew that his *vovó* took her medication at eleven a.m. He would feed her and sit with her by eleven to encourage her to take her pills. She appreciated his comfort and care. They shared the most beautiful bond. Her little star—as she always called David—was right beside her.

The day our trip to France came to an end, my sister promised to pick up my mother's supplements and arrange for the hospital bed to be set up in her apartment. Nurses would be coming three times a day to assist her with basic care. I felt that my mother was in good hands prior to my departure.

For some reason, my mother was adamant that she wanted to accompany us on our ride to the airport, while we preferred that she stay back due to her difficulty walking and standing. She kept insisting that she come with us. There was a sense of urgency in her request, and nothing we could say would change her mind.

By the time we went to the security gate, my mother and David looked at each other one last time and shared a painful goodbye. David hugged my mother tight. Tears erupted from their eyes. They couldn't help but catch the attention of people nearby, some of whom also started to tear up. My sister and I looked at each other, but neither of us wanted to go there. But it seemed like they knew. They knew they were never going to see each other again. This was their last goodbye.

Shortly after we returned home from France, my mother did not sound well on the phone. Her voice was growing softer and weaker, and it got to the point where she could hardly speak on the phone.

It hadn't even been a few weeks since I had returned home, yet there was a strong feeling in my heart telling me that I needed to go back. I did something that I had never done before: I booked a flight back to France for February. I didn't even speak to Tiago about it, I just had an urgent feeling that I needed to do it.

"Did something happen? Did the doctors call you or something?" he asked, concerned and confused.

"No. No one called. I just feel a strong need to go. I cannot question it, but I need to go alone this time," I said convincingly.

I flew back to France in February. Anais picked me up from the airport and brought me to the retirement home. Not wanting to come in with me, she dropped me off and drove away.

As I stepped into the door of the apartment, the first thing I saw was my mother tilting to one side as though she was about to fall. I dropped my things and ran to her side, holding her as she began to tremble. She was barely recognizable. Her elbows and knees were smeared with blood—she was wounded at the joints. Her back looked tiny, she had lost a lot of weight, her skin had yellowed even more, she was bedridden, and she was suffering all alone. When I tried to speak to her, she had difficulty breathing and responding. And her hospital bed—where was it? It was supposed to be set up weeks ago! No wonder she had these wounds, she had to push herself up constantly. But Anais was supposed to take care of her bed.

I opened her fridge and looked around. Where were the supplements? I turned around to look at my mother—she must have been starving. But Anais was supposed to take care of her supplements.

No wonder she drove away after dropping me off. I brought my mother to her bed and placed the emergency necklace around her neck, in case she needed it. I had to leave her for a short period to get a few things from the pharmacy and speak to the director of the retirement home.

As soon as I left her apartment, I erupted in tears. She was in so much discomfort and pain. I hadn't lived in France in so many years, and I wasn't familiar with how the procedures worked for medical assistance inside retirement homes. I spoke to the director, who explained that it could be arranged for my mother to have a hospital bed, an oxygen cylinder, and nurses to check on her three times a day. Once the director shared this information, I followed the steps and began the process right away.

After my talk with the director, I went to the pharmacy to inquire whether there were any supplements under my mom's name.

"Are you the other daughter from Canada?" the pharmacist asked.

"Yes, I am, actually. I just arrived today," I said to her.

"We have been waiting for your sister to pick up these supplements for several days now, but she never came by."

*Anais where have you been? What have you done? How am I leaving the pharmacy with two full bags of supplements? How could you just leave her alone in so much suffering? What is going on, Anais?* These questions were running wild in my mind.

I returned to the retirement home to give my mother her supplements and sat at her bedside. My mother knew that I was upset with my sister for being negligent.

"Émilie, you know the life your sister has. Her husband does not like our family. She does not come that often. When she visits, she washes my laundry, but then has to go. I am a burden. I fought for eighteen months, but I have no strength anymore. You are so far away from me, and you have your own family. Anais is close, but I am too much work. It is time for me to go," my mother said.

"Maman, you are not a burden! Please don't say that! I am here for you. Maman, I am going to give you a nice warm bath. You are going to feel nice and fresh," I said to her.

My mother had no strength to stand, but I washed her on her bed and comforted her. I put cream on her skin and around her wounds. She felt much better, and more relaxed. She was so fragile and needed help. She had taken care of me when I was a little girl, and it was my turn to take care of her. I was going to do all I could to ease her pain and discomfort.

Throughout the night, my mother was thirsty all the time and kept asking to drink. I was so worried that I wouldn't be able to hear her that I started to train myself not to sleep.

Within twenty-four hours, the hospital bed was set up in my mother's room and nurses were visiting her three times a day. To their surprise, many mornings when the nurses were running late, they would find my mother already bathed with cleaned sheets. I needed to make sure my mother was always comfortable. Thankfully, I had learned when I worked at the clinic how to care for someone who is confined in bed. My sister was still nowhere to be seen, and I was angry with her. I felt abandoned by her. We needed to support our mother and make important decisions together, but she wasn't there. I knew I needed to push these thoughts aside and strictly focus on my mother.

Sabrina had dropped by to visit my mother and brought some espresso capsules for me because she knew I hadn't been sleeping. Between the jetlag and my mother needing assistance, I was sleep deprived, but I needed to be awake, so coffee was my companion. That evening, as I began to prepare my mother for bed, she reached out to hold my hand.

"My daughter, please sit. Let's talk," she said softly. I stopped what I was doing and sat with her.

"Émilie, I need to tell you something," she began. "I know many times you wondered whether I loved you less than your sister . . . .I love you the same... I did give more attention to your sister, but I have always been proud of you . . . please know that in your heart. You are a remarkable daughter, and now you are a caring mother and a wonderful wife. You are strong, you are kind, and you have a generous heart. Ever since you were born, I never doubted your strength. When you came into our lives, you threw our world completely upside down. You've always been a firecracker, very straightforward, very honest. I have never doubted your fire, your strength, your tenacity. Maman is and will always be proud of you."

Tears flowed down my cheeks. All my life I needed to hear these words. I kneeled by her bedside and held her hand tightly. In my body, I felt a peaceful feeling flow through me knowing that my mother loved me and was proud of me. I had longed to hear these words. She accepted me, she validated me, she warmed my heart.

"Émilie, you need to let me go. I am ready to go, I am not afraid, but you are. You are the one holding me here. It is time for you to let me go. I can't suffer anymore. I fought with all my might, now I am ready to be at peace," she whispered.

"No, Maman!" I said to her as my voice cracked, "Where are you going? You're staying right here with me!" She gently caressed my head.

"Émilie, I fought . . . with all of my soul. But I am ready to leave this life. Please let me go, set me free. I am ready to go see the light." Her words were slowly fading.

I didn't want to accept her words. I didn't even want to think about her leaving, but I understood what she was saying. Indeed, she had fought furiously all her life, and for the past eighteen months she had suffered and fought this cancer. A moment of silence passed as the heaviness in my heart grew.

"Maman," I whispered, "I don't want you to suffer anymore. If I am the one holding you here, I surrender. I don't want to hold you back anymore. I let you go—go to the light where you will be at peace."

I kissed my mother goodnight and caressed her hand as I watched her fall asleep.

A couple of days later, my mother's condition worsened, and she was no longer able to stay at the retirement home. My mother was placed in a beautiful palliative care unit. The doctors, nurses, and caregivers were beyond wonderful with my mother, and I knew she was going to be taken care of. They had meetings with me every day and offered all kinds of support. The doctors confirmed that my mother had a pulmonary embolism, and it was only a matter of time.

I cancelled my flight back to Toronto. I was going to stay as long as I needed to. My sister had visited my mother in palliative care, but her visits were kept short. She knew I was not happy with her. She knew I had a lot to say. My cousins and all our closest friends came to say their goodbyes to my mother as well. It was only a matter of time until my mother's condition worsened, and I made the decision to put her in a medically induced coma for her comfort. Within a few hours, my mother felt relaxed and was no longer suffering.

The senior physician of the palliative care unit advised me to go home and rest. He was genuinely concerned about me. I had been sleep-deprived for several days. I looked exhausted, and I barely allowed myself to step out to go to the washroom because I was afraid my mother would transition without me next to her. When was at home that night, I called the nurses' station around three a.m. to check on my mother as I lay wide awake in bed. The nurse told me that my mother had a fever that wasn't going down.

On a peaceful mid-February morning, the sun shone its rays in our hearts as doves flew across the sky. The angels welcomed my mother as their newest angel in heaven, honouring her life and her grace.

I waited for sunrise before walking to the hospital. As I started my walk, I felt like someone was around me. It was a weird sensation, like a warm breeze surrounding me. I felt the presence of my *maman*. My cell phone rang at the same time, and it was the same nurse who was calling me to tell me that my mother had peacefully passed away. There was no doubt in my mind that my mother came to me. I felt her.

The pain of losing my mother was so deep, so piercing, that I thought I was going to die. As my mother passed during her sleep, a piece of my heart died with her too. A hole was left inside me.

"Maman, how am I going to live without you? How?" I wept by her side.

I kept holding on to her as long as I could. I just wanted to kiss her, touch her, be with her, tell her I was there. Each teardrop felt like blood coming out of my eyes. I felt like I was going to die from the pain. There was no one to call me "my daughter" anymore, no mother for me to call "*Maman*."

There's a French tradition called *la mise en bière*. It refers to laying the body and closing the coffin. On the morning of my mother's funeral, the closest people to my mother were with me in a small room, where we said our goodbyes to her before they sealed her coffin. My mother wished to have a rose placed on her hands, and I found her the most beautiful red one that looked like it was made of velvet. My family and close friends were all waiting for the last person to show up to honour the conclusion of the tradition. The last person to show up was my sister.

My mother deserved to be honoured and buried with dignity and respect. My sister and I were supposed to pick out roses for her, but Anais never met me at the florist. By the time she showed up to *la mise en bière*, she came by herself, her husband and kids nowhere to be found. For the whole time I'd been in France, it felt like I was an only child. Where was her eldest daughter? *What happened to you, Anais?*

The funeral had a Catholic undertone in honour of my mother's faith. The inside and outside of the chapel was filled with so many people—I had never seen so many people before. Members from the Portuguese community, locals from the Chambéry community, employers of my mother, Madame Bourgeois and so many others whose names I couldn't remember filled the chapel to honour her. She was truly loved.

The funeral Mass began, and the music of Frédéric François's "Ma petite maman" started to play as my mother was carried down the chapel aisle. My mother loved that singer, and the song was beautiful. The casket was surrounded by tall white candles and warm candlelight. The minister shared a few passages from the Bible and delivered a sermon filled with comfort and hope.

Close to the end of the religious ceremony, there were close friends of hers who shared their eulogies. They spoke of their memories with my mother, her strength, her generous heart, her life. I knew my mom had brought so much light to people but listening to the words of others was special. After the last eulogy, my mother was slowly carried out of the chapel to the song of "Ave Maria."

We went to the cemetery after the ceremony, where everyone gathered around my mother's coffin. The minister delivered a final prayer and recited a poem, "Ne restez pas à pleurer," before friends and family began to gently toss white and red roses on my mother's coffin. It was too painful for me to watch my mother descend into the ground, so I turned around to look away. The sound of the coffin descending and hitting the dirt pierced the last unbroken piece of my heart. I had just lost my mother. I felt numb from the deep pain in my heart.

After the funeral procession, my cousin Danny catered a special lunch and invited our close friends and family to celebrate my mom's life at his apartment. We had a lovely lunch together where everyone shared memories of my mother. Madame Minda, Carolina, Sabrina, Madame Re, my aunt, my cousins, and my sister were with me. Revisiting our pasts and sharing our memories brought her presence back to us. It was beautiful.

Madame Re, a close friend and confidant of my mother's, asked to speak with me privately during our lunch at Danny's. Madame Re was the daughter of Papi, the older gentleman my mother took care of back when I was a young girl. Earlier that day, Madame Re shared her eulogy at the ceremony and expressed how my mother took care of her father as though he was her own. When we sat down privately together, Madame Re reached for my hand and extended an envelope to me.

"My little Émilie, here is Papi's last gift to his little Maria," she said, gently caressing my hand. "I know Papi would like me to pay for my Maria's funeral, so allow me to offer your mom this last gift for all she did for us over the years."

"Madame Re, I can't accept this," I said, starting to break down in tears.

"Please Émilie, this is the last gesture that I can honour my Maria with. I am truly going to miss your mother. She was a dear friend of mine, and someone who I was able to trust all these years. She treated my dad very well, and she touched our lives forever," she said. I was certainly not expecting such a kind gesture.

While we were at Danny's apartment, my relatives were worried about me. They knew I had spent the last couple of nights alone in my mother's apartment. I needed to spend time alone with my pain. I needed to be in her space, smell her perfume. I needed to be alone and feel my mom's energy.

Before I left Danny's apartment, I promised my cousins and Aunt Aurora that I would stay with them for the remainder of my trip before I went back to Toronto. They were concerned for me; they did not want me to be alone.

The Sunday morning after the funeral, I asked to my sister to join me at my mother's apartment. We were going to sort out my mother's furniture and belongings, and Aunt Aurora and Madame Minda would accompany me.

When we went to my mother's apartment, I sat along the round table in my mother's living room by the beautiful bay window. We were all waiting for Anais, and my blood started to boil after waiting for her for so long. For the last ten days I had swallowed my words and brushed off my sister's neglectful behaviour because I was too busy focusing all my energy and attention on my mother's final moments.

Anais finally showed up, and she had brought a sturdy cardboard box with her. Madame Minda and Aunt Aurora stood to greet her when she walked in. I really didn't want to speak to her, but I bit the bullet because there were so many questions I wanted to ask before I left for Toronto.

"Anais, why don't you sit down with us?" I asked her tightly.

"Sorry, Émilie, but I don't feel like it," she said with a slightly defensive tone.

"But—"

She turned her back to us and started gathering my mother's belongings, the ones she wanted to take home with her. She barely gave me an opportunity to say anything. I was sick of being ignored. I stood up from the table out of frustration.

"Anais, why have you been absent all this time?" I started to raise my voice. She paused for a moment but proceeded to pick up more of my mother's houseware.

"Anais! Are you even listening to me? *Answer me!*"

She moved the television stand and started disconnecting all the cables behind the TV.

"Excuse me? Where were you to pick up the supplements for Maman? Maman was *starving* when I arrived. And the hospital bed! You promised me on the car ride back to the airport—right before my son said his last goodbye to her—that you would have the hospital bed taken care of. How come you didn't take care of it? I trusted you!"

More ruffling of the television stand, more of Anais's silence.

"When has Maman ever abandoned you? All this time, poor Maman was bedridden and wounded, suffering alone in this apartment. All she needed was basic care! You could have established better care for her while I was gone. Why did you disappear? Why did you leave her alone? You promised me, Anais!"

She moved the television stand back in place and scanned the room for decorations that she could take.

"I called you so many times . . . you ignored my calls and texts. You left me high and dry to take care of Maman while she was vomiting blood. You abandoned me when she needed to go to the hospital. You left me alone with the responsibility to make the decision to induce her into a coma. Even the flowers—where were you to choose the flowers? I took care of it all by myself!"

She started to scatter a bunch of housewares to sort through the ones she wanted and the ones she left behind.

"When did you start lying? How could you promise me all these lies? How could I ever forgive you? How can you live with yourself? *Anais!*"

I took ten long strides toward my sister, pulled her arm back so she could face me, and slapped her. She lost her balance and took a few steps back. She had a look of fear in her eyes. Madame Minda and Aunt Aurora had kept quiet all this time, but they restrained my arms and pushed me against the wall.

My sister stormed out of the apartment with pieces of my mother. I wasn't just grieving the loss of my mother. I had lost my sister too. I was so enraged, so exhausted, so *resentful*. I didn't recognize this girl anymore. I needed to leave. There was nothing left for me in France.

Tiago and David were waiting for me at the airport. I made sure to plan my mother's funeral within a few days of her passing so I could return home as quickly as I could to my boys. David was holding flowers for me, and as soon as he saw me, he rushed to hug me. I kneeled to hug my baby boy tightly—he knew that my mother had passed away. After feeling dead inside all week, I felt a little spark after seeing and hugging my son.

There's a Portuguese custom in which people wear black after someone close to them passes away. I've always loved the colour black, but I thought that wearing a certain colour wasn't a reflection of what went on in your heart. It was only after my mother passed away that I realized I wasn't comfortable wearing any colour besides black. My heart and soul felt entirely black. I had no words to articulate the intensity of my pain. I felt like I was walking in an empty body.

For the first time in our ten years of marriage, Tiago did not know what to do to ease my pain. I wished so many times I could split open my heart and show him how wounded I was inside. I started to live with a mask that hid my vulnerability and shut out the world. But it was still no use; hiding didn't fix anything. Storing our emotions is the worst thing we can do to ourselves.

Trying to share my pain with people around me was like adding salt to a painful battle wound. I sought their comfort, but they looked at me dismissively and reminded me that losing a parent was a part of the cycle of life. They would remind me that I had a family to take care of, and I needed to move on. Move on? These words would just spin me into a dark hole. It was painful to breathe. I still couldn't sleep. I hadn't slept properly in a very long time. It was as though my body had forgotten how to sleep. I asked my doctor to prescribe me something to help me sleep because my mind would replay scenes at night and spiral into a tornado of dark thoughts. I had hit rock bottom. I felt completely trapped in this unbearable pain.

# Epilogue

Four months after my mom's passing, we flew to Portugal in June to vacate the home my mother rented there. Many of her friends in Portugal did not get a chance to say goodbye to her. They all came to pay their respects to me, and they even arranged a ceremonial Mass in memory of my mother.

Being in her house and packing our memories put another emotional strain on me. I was surrounded by her smell, her clothes, her tastes. It was as though I was reliving her death all over again. I felt a piercing pain in my heart, I couldn't breathe, I was unable to let go of her belongings. I wanted her back. I wanted to hold on to her smell a little longer. My heart was broken into pieces and the only strong emotions I felt were deep sadness and anger. I was angry at God for taking her away from me, angry at my sister, angry at myself. I was in so much pain, my body ached, my rheumatoid arthritis flared. There were moments when I wondered whether I would feel whole again. If it weren't for Tiago and David, life would not have been worth living.

Once we emptied the home, Tiago took us to Algarve for a week. The weather there was exceptional, and our hotel was right in front of the beach. Catarina and Beatriz met with us too. They knew how hurt I was, and they were there once again to support me. Since the hotel had a spa, Tiago suggested that I book a relaxing massage with my friends. My back was in knots; my entire body was in pain from carrying the weight of grief.

I booked a spa session for the three of us during our trip. Catarina booked her massage before lunch, mine was after lunch, and Beatriz's was after mine. Before my massage, we ate lunch at a restaurant on the patio. While they were enjoying an ice cream and taking in the surrounding ocean view, I excused myself to withdraw. I gave the excuse that I was going for my massage to leave them behind. The reality was I needed some time alone.

Ever since my mother passed away, I felt guilty for having happy moments. I felt guilty for laughing with my friends. I was trying my best not to show my pain, but at times I felt I was suffocating. More than anything in the world, my mother loved to be in Portugal and I felt guilty for being somewhere she couldn't be. I collected myself and made my way to the hotel spa.

The massage therapist at the spa was dressed in white when she came to greet me. She appeared to be in her fifties. She was warm and considerate during my appointment. When she examined my body while I was face down on the massage table, she felt tightness from all the knots that my body was carrying.

When it was time to flip, she placed her hands around my neck for a moment. Suddenly I felt a painful pressure on my throat, as though she was strangling me. The pain was so intense that I removed her hand and sat upright on the table. I knew she wasn't even touching my neck, but it felt so intense and uncomfortable. Unable to control myself, I erupted with tears and the lady rushed to hand me a box of tissues.

"I felt your pain so deeply . . . I felt the pain in your body. I was pulled to do Reiki on you. I was not touching your throat area, but it was one of your blockages and I was intuitively guided to incorporate energy healing during your massage to help you," she said kindly.

"Reiki? I think I've heard of that before. It has to do with energy, right?" I asked, trying to collect myself.

"Yes! Reiki is energy healing, and you have so much trapped in your throat, so much that you need to say, but you don't. It is one of your energetic blockages. There is a release happening now, but you need to take care of yourself. You need to heal. I can feel the pain that your body carries."

I left the massage room in tears. I couldn't stop crying. I walked up to my room with my sunglasses on. I cried for the rest of the afternoon. Catarina, Tiago, and David had gone to the beach while Beatriz finished her massage. I stayed behind in our hotel suite because I had been crying uncontrollably since my massage. I was intrigued, because a stranger, who knew nothing about my pain, felt it carried in my body. Even from the crying, I felt a sense of lightness in my body, around my throat and chest. It was weird.

After her massage, Beatriz knocked on the door of my hotel room. When I opened it, there she was with her eyes overflowing with tears.

"Jesus, what kind of massage did we get? You too?" I laughed.

"If it was not my experience, I would not believe in it. I would think it was a lie, but I know what I felt. I know this is the truth," Beatriz said.

She walked into my room and sat next to me on the bed.

"I have something to tell you," she began. "I have a message from your mom. The massage therapist could not continue my massage until she delivered this message to me. From the CD player making noise to completely stopping, I knew what I felt. Émilie, I felt your mom in the room. You know how I am—I don't believe in these woo-woo things. For goodness sake, I am a nurse, but I know what I felt. It was definitely your mom."

"What happened in that room?" I asked curiously.

"Your mom knows you love the colour black, but now you are carrying it like a heavy crucifix because of your deep pain. She is very worried about you. You are not well. She is at peace, but you aren't," she explained.

Beatriz held me in her arms, and we cried from her beautiful message. I knew it was my mom. I felt it in my heart.

The following day, Beatriz and I went to talk with the massage therapist, who shared that she was a seventy-year-old Reiki practitioner. She explained to us that she was intuitively guided to do Reiki on me during my massage and it was Beatriz who was chosen to deliver my mother's message. I needed to listen to my mother; after all, she was my guardian angel who was watching over me from above. It was time to take care of myself or I could get sick. I needed to heal. It was time to heal.

At that moment, I knew what my next step needed to be. I admitted that I was indeed not well. Not physically, not emotionally, not mentally. I needed to find my way. I could not continue living in that spiral of darkness. I had already hit rock bottom. Now there was only one way left to go—up! My mom was connected with me, and I knew I was not alone. She was watching over me.

Let the healing journey begin.

# PART II

## FROM MY HEART TO YOURS

I have envisioned writing this book since I was seven years old. Somehow, I knew that it was meant to happen; I believe this book was written in my soul. When I told my Grade 1 teacher that I wanted to write a book about my life, she believed in me and encouraged me. She had faith in me during a time I felt no one else did. She inspired me to read, and she introduced me to the beauty of literature and the art of expression through writing.

In this, the second part of the book, you will journey alongside me as I walk you through the experiences and reflections on my path to self-discovery. The contents of Part II contain a deep reflection of my healing journey, which is strictly based on my personal experiences and from what I have learned through working with clients. The process of writing this book, in and of itself, has established a space to explore and dive even deeper into self-mastery than I ever have before. It called me to look into the pieces of my story and traumas that I still needed to heal from. I never thought that writing would be so emotionally intense. Writing is a profound source of contemplation and reflection, like holding a direct mirror up to my soul.

For the longest time, I struggled to see and embrace my unique gifts. I always felt *less than*. As a child, I aspired to obtain a post-secondary degree. I dreamed of attending a formal education program and graduating with a diploma that had my name on it. As the years passed, I realized that, for me, the idea of achieving this accomplishment had been attached to my self-worth. Though I never received an academic diploma from a post-secondary institution, I acquired certifications later in life, foremost by completing all levels of training to become a Reiki teacher. I also hold a hypnosis certification, meditation instructor certification, and trauma-informed counselling certification. My attachment to acquiring a post-secondary degree used to spiral me into a battle of self-doubt when I struggled deeply to recognize my worth. But writing this book in English, my third language, has been an amazing accomplishment and the bravest act of self-love.

I am a firm believer in the power of sharing our stories. That is why I began this book—to share mine, entirely and authentically. To put myself in the *arena of truth and vulnerability,* as American author Brené Brown explains.

Showing vulnerability is certainly scary and not an easy thing to do, but I strongly felt that putting myself out there, showing my darkest moments, and sharing my deepest reflections could be the starting point for someone else. If telling my story has the power to touch at least one person in this world, then I will have accomplished my goal.

## Just One Step Ahead

I am not a doctor. I don't have a PhD. The contents of Part II are not intended as formal medical or mental health advice. I am certainly not preaching that my way is the right way. I am simply and humbly sharing my own experiences.

What I will be sharing in Part II is not philosophy but the deepest knowledge I gained based on my personal experiences. I hope my words may act as a point of connection in someone else's story. Their own story.

Even though I am often referred to as a healer, I don't usually use that title because I can't heal anyone other than myself. I help others who are on their healing journey to reconnect with their wholeness and find the healer within. I see myself as someone who, after many years of being on my own healing journey, has finally started to connect the points. One might say I have finally found the missing pieces to my puzzle. I facilitate others in their healing journeys, simplifying what is simple. I have learned that being a highly sensitive person is not a curse, but a gift. For most of my life, being highly sensitive was perceived by others as a weakness, but it is actually my biggest strength and a gift that helped me stay in my heart and not become bitter with all the pain I experienced. This sensitivity allowed me to remain compassionate, and now I embody the gift of being highly sensitive as one of my strengths. I am someone who holds space for people to connect with their inner wisdom and unpack their luggage. I am, at times, just one step ahead of the person I am working with. My story allows me to connect and work deeply with clients. After feeling ashamed of my story for many years, I now use it as a beautiful resource to help others connect with their own stories.

Owning my story has freed me and given me a sense of empowerment. I gained my accreditations through real-life experiences, not from academic institutions. My accreditations have all been acquired by attending the highest school of all, the school of life. From hitting rock bottom and finding my way back up to the surface, I have had to learn to stand up, over and over, after each hit to the ground to rebuild my sense of self and heal my bleeding wounds. I have learned how to trust my inner compass. I have taken lessons from each person who has crossed my path. My father has been one of my greatest teachers, as well as my beautiful children and precious mother, whom I hope to make proud each day.

Watching my parents' tenacity as they pushed through challenges has helped me to stand up each time life has tried to knock me down. They experienced challenging upbringings but had the courage to venture to a foreign country in hopes of building a better future for themselves. Their courage helped me seek out the answers I needed to heal myself. My children are my deepest inspiration. I've learned so much about myself simply by watching them live out their own personalities. They are my inspiration to continue this journey of self-discovery and become the best version of myself. I hope that with my own healing, my children will have less baggage to heal from. I hope to empower them to love themselves and cultivate their awareness so their path will be a little lighter than mine.

## The Keys To Turn Within

When we think about spiritual awakenings and the healing journeys, both tend to go hand in hand. When trying to heal, we inherently come to seek a deeper understanding of ourselves. We begin trying to connect with self, since oftentimes our wounds are left open and unhealed simply because we are disconnected from who we are. At the beginning of my healing journey, my natural tendency was to seek guidance from spiritual teachers, healers, and alternative practitioners. I assumed that these practitioners held the right keys to the path set before me, as though they owned the roadmap to my healing path.

Seeking external help is a means of acquiring the tools and resources that eventually guide us to turn inward. They help us before we are ready to look within. Looking within demands a great deal of courage and bravery and can be painfully challenging. There comes a point where we acquire what we know to be enough from outside voices. But once we reach this point, we need to look within and uncover our own unique path to healing. Ultimately, the answers are found within, and we are the only ones with the power to create changes in our lives. You are the only one who holds the keys to the gates of your unique healing journey. You are the architect of your spiritual temple.

I've always liked to look outside of the box and learn about alternative approaches to being that are new to me. For example, after my mom passed away, instead of praying (or "churchin'") my way through the grief, as I was taught growing up, my first response was to connect with a couple of psychic mediums. I wanted to know how she was and receive messages from her. My experiences with the psychic mediums brought me a great deal of comfort at the time. They shared specific details with me that only my mother and I knew of. I believed that the messages I received from the psychic mediums were directly sent from her. It was important for me to know she was at peace.

My mother's message was that she was worried about me, and she needed me to heal. Both mediums delivered the same message to me. I kept hearing that I was meant to help people and that I had a purpose, which always brought me back to a similar message that I received on the night I attempted to end my suffering. They explained that I had healing hands and an amazing gift, and that I was going to use them later in life in my service to others. But initially I had no idea what this meant, "to help people and find my purpose." I felt confused about it. I needed to do it for myself. And yet, it also seemed clear to me that I needed to heal and begin my spiritual journey.

## The Starting Point

It was time. I knew I needed to work on myself. I was a mess. My emotions were intense and turbulent. It was almost as if all that was done to me, all the people who did wrong by me, surfaced. All I could feel was anger. I was mad at the world. I was mad at my father for being alive, and angry with my sister for the way she handled things with our mother. These were my starting points. I began by sorting through all these strong emotions and allowing myself to grieve.

People around me tried their best to help, but by no fault of their own their help only added to my pain. People offered me advice to the best of their abilities, given their own conditioning and traumas, and according to where they were personally in their own journeys at the time. They said things like, "Move on with your life," "You are a wife and mother; you need to move on and take care of your husband and your son," and, "Your mom's passing is a part of the cycle of life, and you need to accept it." Accept what? When someone you love deeply passes away, you can only move forward but you can't move on. It was almost as though my tears were making them uncomfortable, and the best way to avoid the discomfort was by shutting me down. It made me feel like my pain was insignificant, and that grief had an expiration date. These words felt more like dismissive demands than advice. For the first time in my life, I locked my pain and my words away, and I felt isolated from others. I even struggled to articulate my pain to Tiago. So many times, I wished that I could just open my heart so he could see the hole I felt and carried.

I was actively reading books by Deepak Chopra, Wayne Dyer, and Louise Hay. I was committed to understanding the connection between mind, body, and spirit. Along with the reading I was doing, my experience with rheumatoid arthritis began to help me understand the ways in which our emotional state can be highly connected to our physical health.

Research from David R. Hawkins, an American psychiatrist, shows that our emotions have measurable energy. Our emotions are powerful. They can foster or negate cell life, as he explains in *Power vs. Force*. In his remarkable groundwork, he shows that the measurable energy of someone increases as the person experiences more positive emotions. His most striking find, to me, is that cells die when the logarithmic scale—that is, the measurable energy level—is below 200. Emotions like hate, guilt, and shame affect the logarithmic scale. His findings show how vital positive emotions are in regulating our health.

At the time, I knew my rheumatoid arthritis was flaring and I needed to help myself. My hormones were completely off, and my stress level was very high. A friend of mine recommended her healer and medical medium. Vasco, the healer, was very direct and open with his communication. In one of our conversations, he made it clear that if I did not reduce my stress, I would eventually become physically ill, just like my mother. He made it clear that his role was only to assist me; he did not perform miracles. I needed to make the choice to help myself. He said that my healing was uniquely in my hands and no one else's. The process would not be easy. It was difficult to hear that, but I knew he was right.

While I was working with the medical medium, David and I were working with a psychotherapist to help him process his grief. He suffered the loss of his grandmother at a very young age, and I wanted to make sure his emotional needs were met. I wanted to help him process the loss of his grandmother and support him in his healing. He was grieving as well. I was meeting with this psychotherapist every other week. However, I knew inevitably that I needed to go deeper energetically, emotionally, mentally, and spiritually. I needed to understand my emotions on a deeper level and work with them, not shut them down. I needed to allow myself to feel so I could heal.

"Who am I?" I wondered for the first time. Throughout my life, I was a daughter to my mother whom I needed to protect and advocate for. Now that I had lost my mom, I no longer needed to wear this hat. For the first time it felt as though I could turn my fight or flight mode off. I really didn't know who I was anymore. I was lost, I felt like an orphan. I had no one to call me "my daughter." I walked around with a hole in my heart that at times felt so ironically heavy.

Some more questions arose: What kind of mother and role model did I want to be for David? How did I want to show up in the world? As a child, many times I would imagine my own death and funeral. I never feared my own death, only the death of those whom I loved. I had always wanted to leave my mark on this world. I had always wanted to be remembered for being someone who brought good to the world. These were the questions and hopes that kept circling my mind. I wanted to release the anger that was consuming me.

I wanted to learn to do better for myself, for my family, and for the world. I believe that we have the power to impact the world with our own healing and transformation. I have always been a fan of Oprah Winfrey, and I will forever be grateful for *The Oprah Winfrey Network* (OWN). Her Masterclasses and *Super Soul Sundays* were my free therapy. Whenever I tuned in, it felt like the OWN Network had prepared a message that was specifically designed for me to hear. I knew that there were no accidents, only synchronicities. One episode featured John Diaz, a survivor of the 2000 Singapore Airlines crash. Diaz did not consider himself a spiritual person until his near-death experience in the crash. He set the life-transforming scene for viewers as he described the inside of the plane as resembling a scene out of Dante's *Inferno*. The plane was in flames after the explosion, and people's bodies were burning in their seats. He witnessed what he described to be "auras coming out of people's bodies. Some brighter than others."

From surviving his near-death experience, he explained that he developed a greater sense of compassion toward others, a belief in the afterlife, and a newfound commitment to his own life. He explained that moving forward from the incident, he would like to live his life in such a way that his aura would be as bright as it could be when it was his time to leave Earth. His message resonated with me deeply, as it affirmed my belief that when our body dies, the soul lives on. It also prompted my own reflection on how I would like to live my life. I, too, wanted to live a life that would expand my aura to be as bright. I wanted to have a positive influence in this world.

At times, we need a little push from the Universe. My push came on a freezing Sunday at the end of 2013. I was skating with my boys when I slipped, hitting my head on the ice. The back of my head banging against the ice produced a shockingly loud sound that matched the intensity of the pain I felt. I thought for sure that I had cracked my skull open. I was rushed to the emergency room. Seven hours and a CT scan later, I was discharged with a concussion and an acute neck injury. Thankfully, I had no internal bleeding, but I needed to rest in order to heal.

A couple of days later, while I was resting in bed with my eyes closed after the injury, I heard a voice softly whisper the word, "Reiki." Despite my eyes being closed, I saw the word "Reiki" appear before me. I knew that this was a divine message, and I needed to trust it. My next step was Reiki energy healing. I felt that I finally understood the message given about my healing hands. I was not sure where this path was going to lead, but I needed to listen.

## Our Bodies Remember

What is Reiki? It comes from the Japanese word *Rei*, meaning, "universal energy (universal consciousness)," and *Ki* (also *Chi* in Chinese, or *Prana* in Sanskrit) meaning "life force energy." Reiki has many branches, but generally it can be explained as a gentle, non-invasive, natural energy approach that promotes self-regulation in the body. Reiki helps to unlock the flow of energy to restore inner balance, which is also known as "homeostasis." Every atom, every cell, and every tissue are composed of energy. Life force energy nourishes organs and cells, supporting the body's vital functions.

Reiki helps unlock the flow of energy in our seven main energy centres, known as *chakras*. The Sanskrit word "chakra" means "wheel" or "disk." Chakras are like spinning vortexes of energy. These energy centres store our thoughts, emotions, feelings, and experiences. They are connected to our massive nerve centres in the body. And the chakras are connected to our major organs and our psychological, emotional, and spiritual well-being.

Our traumas and emotions are trapped in our bodies, as Western scientific research has come to recognize. In Bessel van der Kolk's *The Body Keeps Score: Brain, Mind, and Body in the Healing of Trauma*, van der Kolk shares an incredible testimonial on how our traumas and emotional stresses are stored in our bodies. I felt that taking a natural energy healing approach was the next step on my healing journey. Just looking at the chakras or energy centres system gives us a *roadmap* to help us see and experience the interconnectedness of our anatomy, our mindset, our emotions, and our energy. Everything is connected.

When I had my first experience with Reiki in Portugal during 2012, my throat—the fifth energy centre—was blocked. From a physical perspective, I always held my stress in my neck and shoulders. At the time, I had a very small, enlarged lymph node on my neck that was kept under supervision by a specialist.

Looking at what was happening specifically on my neck from a spiritual perspective helped me understand how the throat chakra was related to consciousness and higher forms of communication. To have this chakra balanced is to speak your inner truth. It is not about speaking your mind; rather, it is about listening, speaking, and expressing yourself from a higher form of communication. At the time, I had trouble expressing my feelings and emotions. Since I was a little girl, I had never asked for help, I didn't even know how. I had a hard time even saying the words "I need help." Expressing my needs was something I battled with all my life. Also, as previously mentioned, I felt locked in the pain of my mother's passing. I found myself constantly swallowing my words. The only thing I managed to communicate successfully was my anger. I spoke from my ego, which was guided by pain, sadness, and grief. Even though I was always speaking what I perceived being the truth, my delivery was certainly wrong, and I was not aware of my inner truth. I needed to explore what was going on with my other chakras because I knew there were more blockages in my energetic field. Knowing that our body keeps score, I knew my rheumatoid arthritis related to emotional pain, so I was determined to heal by examining the root cause of my pain.

## From Client To Practitioner To Teacher

In early 2014, I dove into studying Reiki and took the required courses to become a Reiki practitioner. The course material resonated with me deeply, so much so that my learning bled into my own self-healing in a remarkable and profound way. I became more in tune with my body. I found myself truly listening to my body for the very first time in my life.

Studying Reiki and practicing it on myself helped me to better understand energy. When the energy felt locked in my body, I learned to listen to the energy. I began to see dance in a new light as well. I understood why dancing was a cathartic experience for me. Movement, like dance, helps to move energy that is stuck in our bodies. Understanding the mind, body, and spirit connection helped me reconnect with my energy, and consequently it made me more aware of how sensitive I have always been to the energy of others.

Little by little, I unveiled my wounds and a deeper understanding of my body, ultimately expanding my level of self-awareness and consciousness. The third chakra—the solar plexus—is connected to the stomach, liver, and pancreas. The solar plexus was also a place of blockage for me. No surprise there, as I always had issues with my stomach. From a spiritual perspective, this energy centre relates to personal power, self-worth, and transformation. From being self-conscious of my body to underestimating my own abilities, I always had issues with my self-esteem. My father tore my self-esteem apart at a very young age. When my solar plexus was blocked, I carried expressions of anger, fear, and hate. Oh, did I ever feel them! I was so angry, like I was on fire on the inside. I knew I needed to forgive my father, my sister, and myself, but I was in so much pain at the same time that it seemed like anger was the only thing I could feel. Yet, I knew I wanted to be free from these negative emotions. I *had* to be free. They were consuming me.

There is a tremendous amount of power in forgiveness. Forgiveness is the most precious gift you can offer yourself. Forgiveness can have a deep benefit to our mental, emotional, and spiritual health. In psychology, forgiveness is "an emotional and cognitive process that is characterized by the releasing of anger to bring oneself a sense of peace." To be human is to have a story and, at times, we get stuck in the narratives and the stories we tell ourselves. We are creatures that not only live out stories, but also create webs of stories in our minds. Our minds are good at this. We project our fears onto others, especially when the lens we project it from is filled with the scratches from our own wounds. We see the wrongdoings and imperfections of others and our own unmet expectations, which often leaves us feeling disappointed.

For me, the first step to forgiveness was to acknowledge that forgiving my sister did not mean her wrongdoings did not exist. On the contrary, forgiving Anais meant that I no longer needed to be a prisoner to negative emotions. The negative emotions no longer had the power to control me. Forgiveness was not a gift to her, but a gift for me.

From diving into the study of trauma, I navigated my own healing journey by considering Anais's behaviour and understanding why she acted the way she did. Before she was six years old, Anais was emotionally and physically abused by my father. Consequently, Anais developed coping mechanisms as a child to deal with her pain, a natural reaction for anyone facing traumas or whose needs were not met as a child. As a child, she used "dissociation" as a survival tactic to cope. Dissociation helps individuals cope with traumatic experiences. Since the mind and body are overwhelmed from the traumatic experience, we tend to dissociate ourselves to ease the immediate feelings we are experiencing.

When my mother was diagnosed with cancer, the coping mechanisms Anais used as a child stayed with her during adulthood. Anais was overwhelmed with my mother's cancer and with the idea of losing her that she neglected the situation to help her. Instead, Anais created a mental escape to cope with the pain she was experiencing. It was a protective response. Not being around my mother and not witnessing her health degrade day by day made the reality of my mother's condition almost fictional for her. In my study of trauma, I learned that disassociation is a common response for people who suffer deep traumas. In considering Anais's behaviour during my mother's final years, I was able to unpack the pain and anger that her neglect added onto me.

After my mother's passing, Anais sought healing through therapy. She wanted to process the guilt she was experiencing for the way she had handled my mother's illness. She couldn't even understand why she acted the way she did. Through her therapy sessions, she eventually reached the same conclusions as I had about her coping mechanisms and behaviour. Listening to Anais's conclusions and understanding where she was coming from was a tremendous gift and a powerful confirmation for me to let go of my anger towards Anais.

## Finding Peace In The Grey Area

All my life, I have felt strongly about my beliefs and justice, as you may have concluded from some of my life experiences in Part I. I must confess, along with this strong sense of justice came rigidity at times. I often experienced a lack of understanding of the full picture. The experience with Anais taught me to see beyond black and white and to look at the full picture instead. Our traumas have the power to throw us into disequilibrium for our entire lives if we don't help ourselves. We all have our story, one that I believe can powerfully influence our choices according to the pain we carry. Our coping mechanisms alter our perceptions, our behaviour, and our reactions. Our childhood tendencies and experiences bleed into adulthood, whether we are open to seeing it or not. As Dr. Gabor Maté explained on the film 'The Wisdom of Trauma' "Trauma is not what happened to you, it's what happens inside you as a result of what happened to you."

Humbly, I can tell you that understanding this piece about trauma was a game changer in my life. Understanding that we carry generational traumas is a way to look at our lives, our patterns, and the conditioning given to us from our parents, our culture, and society. Understanding that we all carry some level of trauma, and being conscious of that every day, is a tremendous step in our healing journey. For example, it taught me to not take everything so personally because everyone is battling with something in their lives. Being able to come to a place where I try to witness the experience, I have with others has been liberating for me.

We carry baggage that is not even ours, yet it still affects us. My mother carried so much pain that was hardly her own. She carried traumas that were passed down by her mother, who lost her husband during the Second World War. From the time my mother was five years old, she grew up to be deeply depressed.

During my mother's upbringing in a traditional Portuguese household, mental health was culturally dismissed and misunderstood.

Being Portuguese myself, I have observed that living with mental health challenges was often seen as being weak in our community.

Taking antidepressants has often been understood to be an acceptable mental health treatment but speaking to a therapist often meant that you were seen as crazy. It is common for Portuguese men to soothe their pain by turning to alcohol. Portuguese women who take medication are not condemned for doing so but talking about their emotions to someone would make them "weak" or "crazy." These culturally acceptable "treatments" for addressing mental health are conditioning people to restrict themselves from asking for help.

Unfortunately, the stigma surrounding mental health treatments and the mentality that seeking professional help makes someone crazy extends to many other cultures as well. Most of the time, the need to take care of our mental health and our emotional hygiene is still dismissed. People surrender to the notion that "life is life, and there is nothing we can do about it." I still witness the stigma in generations that are younger than my mother of people continuing to live with the fear of being judged or labelled, or people being marginalized by their families and communities for trying to address their mental health. Their coping mechanism becomes staying unconscious, where they choose addiction to soothe their pain because it is more acceptable and familiar. Consequently, it can be challenging for most of us to take charge of our lives and heal on our own terms because of cultural constructs and the bounds of society as a whole

We need to be able to look at mental health as we do physical health. We need to push these unrealistic and destructive barriers away from our children, so they can carry a new approach in our society where mental health is simply health.

## Journeying Through the Adaptations to Rediscover Self

The concept of generational trauma and its connection to home environments has been studied and explained by many experts. They explain that children pick up on the stresses of their parents, influencing the developing child's nervous system before and after birth.

My mother was depressed and highly stressed while I was in the womb and onwards. My basic emotional needs were not met as a child, regardless of the physical and emotional abuse that I experienced from my father. I understand now that I created an adaptation of myself due to the projections of others and to survive, and I created coping mechanisms to deal with the pain. The way we see things in life and the perception of ourselves is impacted during our childhood. We are not our personalities, nor are we the adaptations or the coping mechanisms we created to survive. Our true nature is beyond that, but it is our responsibility to journey toward rediscovery and reconnection with who we truly are.

In late 2014, I connected with my healing on another level. I was reminded of the phrase, "Practice what you preach." After two years of trying, I got pregnant with our second child. What a blessing! My early pregnancy, however, was challenging. I had an infection and I had to take strong antibiotics. Since my mother's death in 2012, I'd had an enlarged lymph node on my neck. I never allowed doctors to touch it because it was under two centimetres in diameter, and I didn't feel it was a concern. My reasoning for having an inflamed lymph node came down to the idea that I had a weak immune system due to my rheumatoid arthritis.

During the initial stages of pregnancy, the lymph node was stable, and I assumed that the lump was normal, as it was not growing. Within the first eleven weeks of my pregnancy, however, the lump grew from 1.9 cm to 5.9 cm. I had what looked like an egg on my neck. Understandably, the specialist overseeing my case was concerned. He placed a camera inside my nose, which showed more lymph nodes on each side of my throat. My heart felt tight. My specialist and the four interns wanted to perform a biopsy immediately after the ultrasound, but I had a strong feeling, an inner knowing, that the biopsy was not the route for me to take. In response to this strong feeling I excused myself, refused the biopsy, and walked out of the room.

Tiago was silent. I could read the fear in his eyes. But I figured, at eleven weeks pregnant, what would the doctors do if there was something wrong anyway? Honestly, I did not want to find out. I knew I needed to take a visit to Vasco, the energy healer and medical medium I had worked with after my mother passed away.

For the first time in three years, Vasco was silent when he saw me. He maintained his silence for a peculiar amount of time before he broke with an explanation of what he sensed. He sat in front of me and explained that my blood seemed very weak. He explained that the lymphatic system is part of our immune system. The lymphatic system includes a network of lymph vessels and lymph nodes. Lymph vessels are a lot like veins. Whereas veins collect and carry blood throughout the body, lymph vessels carry the clear watery fluid known as the lymph.

Vasco believed that the fluid in my lymph node was not draining the way it was supposed to, and we needed to aid the drainage process. He proposed that we treat it with a natural approach, with supplements like Noni juice and chlorophyll, along with daily healing sessions with him for two weeks.

Vasco also instructed me to stay away from electronics because of the radiation, which was something he believed was weakening my immune system. I used to sleep with my phone right beside my bed, but I stopped to limit my radiation exposure. I needed to start lymphatic massages to help with the fluid drainage. The most important part was *me*, my work. I needed to take care of myself so he could help me. I needed to practice self-healing on myself as well. Most importantly, I needed to master my thoughts. If I was fearful and riddled with negative thoughts, then the treatment would not work. I had no other choice but to do my inner work.

Well, this was it. I was faced with a circumstance that mandated me practicing what I was preaching to those I worked with. I taught about the power of our mind, the power of our faith, and the need to access our inner pharmacy. There was a beautiful quote from Caroline Myss that came to mind during this moment of realization, it is framed and hanging on my office wall for clients to see: "The soul always knows what to do to heal itself, but the challenge is to silence the mind." It was made clear that I needed to silence my mind to access healing. I could not surrender to fear, or I would be sending negative signals to my cells.

My mind, body, and soul needed to work together to ensure a smooth pregnancy, so I could be healthy for my family. I also had a deep conversation with God, just the two of us. I refused to believe He was going to take me away from my son and my unborn child. It was not my time to go. I came to the conclusion that this was my test: you can only teach to others what you have learned for yourself. I chose to see this moment as a lesson I needed to learn so I could authentically assist others.

## The Power of Visualization

Following Vasco's instructions, I knew in my heart that he was right. Every day, I spent time working seriously on myself. I performed self-Reiki, and I began using visualizations and affirmations. I started with visualizing my lymphatic system. I pictured each lymph node and the clear fluid draining out of it. I practiced gratitude and started thanking every organ and cell for the amazing hard work they do in keeping me alive.

Every time a dark cloud of fear appeared over me; I shifted my attention to what I wanted versus what I didn't. I wanted the lymph node to get smaller and restore its health. I started creating boundaries to protect myself from the negative comments surrounding my decision. Some people around me had thoughts and opinions that were ultimately negative, and I could not allow any kind of negative energy to penetrate my efforts. I started hiding my neck with scarves and turtlenecks to avoid unwarranted comments.

I understood the power of visualization with my own personal experience after reading about it from Louise Hay and Dr. Joe Dispenza's books. Once again, I trusted my intuition and my inner wisdom with the decision I made, even though my efforts seemed irrational to those around me. They made it clear with some hurtful comments. I believed that taking this energy-focused approach to my health was the best course of action for me and my baby. Vasco assured me that everything would be back to normal before my baby was born. I surrendered and trusted this process with all my might. With time, I could feel the lymph node on my neck slowly reduce as I continued to follow Vasco's natural approach. By August 2015, we welcomed a healthy and strong baby girl, and the enlarged lymph node was almost unnoticeable.

The negativity of others touches us energetically. Those who have the tendency to consistently pour their negative energy onto others makes for what we call "energy suckers." I have learned that negative energy can come in the form of blame, projection, and manipulation. From paying attention to patterns of negative energy, I learned to watch out for those who consistently, sarcastically, and insensitively make judgmental critiques about other people's choices, especially when their journeys do not align with those who they are commenting on.

Often people are unconscious of their projection onto others. They are not even aware of the heavy energy they carry. We cannot control the awareness of others, but we can control our exposure to negativity. We can love family members or friends and at the same time learn to create healthy boundaries. Honouring ourselves and our needs is important, and it is perfectly fine to distance ourselves from people whose wounds bleed onto others. It reduces unnecessary bullshit in our lives.

Negativity can spring from projecting fears and stories onto others, either consciously or unconsciously, or minimizing another person's experiences and feelings. During our healing journey it is important to monitor what we listen to, including who we spend time with, what we watch on television, and what we consume on social media. If we spend most of our time surrounded by negativity, we remain out of balance.

Here I will list some exercises that I personally learned and use. For years now, I have shared with my clients and students. Grounding techniques can be useful for various intentions, especially to protect your energy.

### Grounding exercise

Sit with your back straight. This will promote a healthy flow of energy through your spine.

Place your feet flat on the ground. Take three deep breaths. Breathe in through your nose, counting to four slowly. Feel the air enter your lungs. Begin to exhale slowly for a count of four. You can repeat this cycle three times.

Visualize roots stemming from the base of your spine, travelling through your legs to your feet and down to Mother Earth. Imagine yourself positioned like a majestic tree, strongly rooted and grounded.

### Protection exercise

Visualize a beautiful bubble of light surrounding you. Picture it completely sealing your body and energy, from under the soles of your feet to the very top of your head.

This visualization is your energy shield meant to protect you from heavy energy. You may picture this bubble containing one layer or multiple layers of colour. What colours resonate with you right now? What colours embody your power? Add on the colours to your visual bubble, as you see fit.

We all have co-workers, friends, or family members whose energy can be challenging to deal with. Picture your unique bubble of light or ground yourself to Mother Earth before the next time you have an encounter with an energy sucker. These simple exercises are meant to help us enter these situations with a greater sense of centredness, calmness, and empowerment.

Through this experience, I had been able to tap into the inner pharmacy and intelligence that we all possess. I was humbly reminded of the power of our minds. I was reminded that our healing journey is an ongoing one.

## Nourishing Self First

Self-awareness. Self-love. Self-worth. These were the words I needed to experience to activate a deep transformation within myself. Collectively, we all have the capacity to access our inner intelligence. When we tap into our inner intelligence, the body naturally knows how to heal itself. I knew and experienced this inner pharmacy. I know I can trust it. I experienced its healing benefits with my rheumatoid arthritis and my enlarged lymph node. Yet, there was an important piece missing in this complex yet dazzling puzzle of my healing journey.

Self-love and self-esteem are two elements of my healing journey that I found exceptionally challenging, especially as I started my Reiki practice with clients. As an empath and a highly sensitive person, it wasn't easy to understand and practice the universal law of giving and receiving. All I knew how to do was give myself completely, without receiving. Unconsciously, I was experiencing burnout. Although I had already worked through some major pieces of my trauma, I knew there was still something missing, and it had to do with the way I treated myself. I spent my life believing that others needed more help, attention, and devotion than I did. This limiting belief showed up in my private practice as well. I had a tough time charging people adequately for my services and managing how much additional time I was spending with them. Consequently, to my little self-worth, I was not able to limit my energy or value my time to be fair to myself. I was not in balance.

My clients were happy and highly satisfied with my work. My clients are based on referrals, the most beautiful compliment you can receive, but I was still battling with a sense of self-worth.

I have been grateful to witness and be a part of many journeys. I experienced, and continue to experience, countless transformative moments with my clients and students. The outside praises for my amazing work were music to my ears, but they were not powerful enough to penetrate my heart. Admittedly, the low voice in me persisted, "You are not enough," despite all the praises and compliments.

The Universe always has our back, and it always sends signs to reassure us of that. We simply need to listen. During one instance, my sign from the Universe came in the form of another certification to take part in. I enrolled in an eight-month program to become a certified Primordial Sound Meditation teacher with The Chopra Centre, which was founded by Dr. Deepak Chopra and Dr. David Simon. The very first step was receiving my personal mantra, calculated, and based on the day, time, and where in the world I was born. "Mantra" is a Sanskrit word that translates in English as "tool or vehicle of the mind." My personal mantra doesn't hold a meaning but a vibration, the one that the world was making when I was born. After receiving my personal mantra, I committed myself to meditate for an hour each day. Indeed, having one of my spiritual teachers, Deepak Chopra, sign my certification felt completely surreal, but it wasn't the most important part of the certification. I met beautiful people through my studies whom I will forever be grateful for. That was certainly another gift.

However, the most precious gift was finding myself. Through my daily meditation practice, I learned that I am not my body, and I am certainly not my story or my limitations. I am a being of infinite possibilities. Through the program, I learned to nurture the most important relationship that one can possibly have in this life: the relationship with self. The relationship we have with ourselves impacts all other relationships in our lives. Through my meditation practice, I reconnected with who I am, my true essence. I came to understand who we really are; that is, beings of infinite possibilities and pure potentiality. Our true essence is pure love and consciousness that is buried under our conditioning and under the 50 to 80,000 thoughts we have in a day.

Meditation is our way back home. Meditation does not create silence but reconnects us with our inner silence. Finding and nurturing a relationship with myself helped me understand the importance of self-care. To me, self-care looks like making sure I am nourished first so I can hold space for others without depriving myself. I did this by creating and maintaining healthy boundaries in my work and in my personal life.

## Stepping Into My Power

When I reached forty years old, I felt more alive than ever. I embraced my forties with a great deal of happiness. I finally understood what "stepping into my power" really meant. I felt alive and light, lighter than I felt at twenty years old. It was almost as if I was seeing myself in a whole new light, as I finally believed that simply being who I am is enough. Who we are is not what we do. We are not merely a reflection of our titles, our material possessions, or our academic degrees. Those are society's labels and projections of who we should be. They are not the whole of who we are.

I will explain further using the animated *Kung Fu Panda* movie. In the film, a bumbling panda and a kung fu enthusiast become the chosen dragon warriors whose duty is to protect the valley and the villagers from harm. The master himself is in disbelief that a panda is the chosen one due to his lack of training and understanding of the art of kung fu. An older master reminds him that there is no accident, only synchronicities. The dragon warrior is gifted with the dragon scroll. Legend has it that the scroll carries the secret that the dragon warrior needs to fight any enemy and save the valley. When the panda opens the dragon scroll, there is no secret. He only sees his reflection. *He* is the special ingredient. When he finally steps into his power, using only his own abilities, he successfully saves the valley.

I had watched this movie several times with my son, yet only a few years ago I understood the message unfolding on a deeper, personal level. In that moment, I made a shift toward believing in myself and recognizing that I am valuable. Once I felt and fully embraced my unique self as valuable, I started to see greater changes in my life. This shift in my mindset released an immense heaviness from my body, and the fear of failure began to escape me. You can't fail in being who you are because there is no one else like you! We are the special ingredients needed in our lives. Let these words sink into your hearts. My meditation practice, day by day, helped me step into my power. For me, meditation felt like coming back home. Every meditation session is like dipping into a sea of infinite possibilities.

Meditation and Reiki are much more than modalities for me. They are a way of life. I believe you need to consciously embrace and be aware of yourself every day. It involves mastering oneself through daily practice, especially to work with others on navigating their own healing journey. I made a promise to myself years ago when I started working with clients. I committed to heal myself continuously and remain humble and open to always keep learning.

**Players on the Spiritual Playing Field**

People like me are often called "healers," "wellness coaches," "spiritual coaches," etc. These are only titles, but they come at times with the projections and expectations that we are gifted with the answers because we are in the spiritual field. But the reality is, we are on the same journey as those we work with. It is our responsibility to continuously work on ourselves. It is our duty to resist the idea that we are suddenly gifted and capable of downloading from the Divine, as if we no longer need to look within ourselves. There is no boot camp for enlightenment. Our life journey is the only way to it.

When working with others, practitioners in the varying fields of spirituality need to maintain a clear distinction between the messages received from divine forces (for example, guides and guardian angels), and the messages delivered from the ego. It is important that we remain sensitive to the fact that we work with some of people's most deep-seated wounds and vulnerabilities.

I firmly believe that in the spiritual realm, we practitioners carry the same ethical weight as any other scope of practice. In my energy work, I have come to understand the importance for energy practitioners to work from a trauma-informed perspective, for example. In doing so, we must take into consideration the mental and emotional health of our clients who are seeking our help from this specific lens. So many people are desperate to find ways to ease their pain and suffering. Someone can be re-traumatized, meaning that their pain can be aggravated depending on the response given to them. People searching for guidance in their spiritual path can be vulnerable. The well-being of others needs to be the single most important and constant priority in our work. For me, it means always staying in the lane of my expertise.

Here is where the question of malpractice arises. Malpractice breeds discreditation in fields of spiritual work and mocks ancient traditions, practices, and wisdoms, which are integral to the integrity of the work that we, the so-called teachers, healers, and practitioners, commit ourselves to throughout this ongoing healing journey. As a sign of respect for each person we encounter in and outside of our work, we must remain humble and not take advantage of people's vulnerabilities by looping them into our own biased perceptions.

People working in spiritual fields need to be always conscious of their own baggage. We must refrain from projecting our own beliefs onto clients, because what may be freeing for us may be limiting for our clients. Taking my own experience as an example, I will never recommend to those suffering from autoimmune disorders to stop taking their prescribed pharmaceutical drugs. I work with many clients who take a strong pharmaceutical protocol, and my work is to assist them in their journey, not to tell them what to do. My personal choice and beliefs have absolutely no place in my work with people.

Reiki is not about prescribing or curing. A Reiki practitioner cannot heal you. You are the only one who has the power to heal yourself!

## Healing is Continuous Work

Over the years, I have encountered many clients who have been misguided in their spiritual work, leaving them hurt and skeptical toward energy healing or spiritual approaches. It has made me take a stand and confirm my belief in the importance for spiritual practitioners to remain humble in their own journeys.

Unfortunately, we live in a fast-food society, and this is seen in the spiritual realm as well. Especially with the pandemic, we experienced a huge surge in the wellness community, with overnight "spiritual healers." For instance, Reiki courses are often offered and taught in only a few hours, and the students are left with a little basic understanding and little practice. It is believed that Reiki dates to about 2,500 years ago but, Dr. Mikao Usui, discovered it and started teaching it in the 1920s. There are five pillars in Reiki:

Just for today, I will be peace

Just for today, I will be joy

Just for today, I will be grateful

Just for today, I will earn a living honestly and decently

Just for today, I will show love and respect for every form of life

It is known that Dr. Usui believed that Reiki was a spiritual path and a daily and continuous journey to self-development and self-mastery. He taught his students to practice healing on themselves and focus on their spiritual development. Reiki practice and meditation were taught, to maintain a calm and peaceful mind. Something that needs to be practiced daily, our spiritual path never ends, there is no diploma or graduation. It is a journey. For us to be "clear channels" when offering Reiki to others, we need to develop our spirituality first, build a strong spiritual temple, and be able to maintain a calm and peaceful mind so we are not attached to our ego but connected with universal love. That can't be taught in a few hours; it must be practiced daily. Our ability to serve and offer Reiki to others relies on our spiritual practice. Personally, Reiki is a way of living, and these five pillars are my guiding light.

We must remain teachable and continue our own healing. We can only serve others if we are healthy ourselves. In the context of Reiki, for instance, it is crucial that Reiki practitioners detach themselves from their ego in their spiritual work to be able to tap into universal love to hold space for others. This connection to our highest forms of consciousness is an active and continuous journey, and essential when working with other souls.

## Discernment Through Questioning

I can humbly share that the Universe will continue to throw circumstances in front of us to push us further in our journey. The Universe will call on us to question whether our wounds are healed, and our lessons are learned. What is coming next was a painful but great experience that allowed me to look deeper at what was needed.

Through a common connection, I had met with someone who is seen as a spiritual teacher. This person provided me with the validation little Émilie craved. In the beginning, this individual did an awesome job validating me and making me feel seen. It felt so special and rewarding to be on the receiving end of these remarks, as I truly believed that I had found someone genuinely interested in my work and my approach.

However, being who I was and having survived my father's abuse, I have grown to pay attention to people's words and actions, especially when they are not in harmony with their words. I started to notice a visible disconnect between the two, and I couldn't help but seek the truth. I started questioning this individual's intentions, and, to my surprise, the answers I received sounded all too familiar, as though they were echoing my father's. I was told that the Devil was tempting me for even questioning this individual. And just like that, I ended up back in my childhood. I could not believe what I was hearing. Every word was piercing. From being told that I was "the amazing Émilie, the gifted and needed healer," to suddenly being told that I was someone who was "tempted by Satan," who was "missing the spiritual truth," made me feel like my father was speaking to me again.

Spirituality is not a religion of rights and wrongs. Spirituality is a personal design. There is not one spiritual path that is greater than the others, because we are all spiritual beings. Spirituality is connected to finding our own path, which is unique and will look different for every one of us. I had a difficult time letting go of this individual's words. Just like my father, this person proved to be disingenuous, and went into attack and defense mode when questioned. I found myself spiralling back to the same feelings of never being enough that my father triggered in me. This interaction reopened a wound that was not fully healed.

## Protecting My Power

In life, you always have a choice: you can hide behind a protective veil or lose yourself and hurt others in the process. Reflecting on this process, I suddenly realized that I too had created stories in my head surrounding this person. I had projected my expectations onto this individual. I sought out validation from my father, this individual, and all those who were teachers or authority figures in my life.

It became apparent to me that I had given this person too much of my power. I was expecting this person to validate me and praise my service to others—my life's work. This moment was a breakthrough for me because I knew this situation was calling me to address a wound that needed to be healed, and I could not be more grateful for it.

Around the same time, a famous American author landed on my social media page. I had the opportunity to exchange some thoughts with him. He motivated me to restart writing the book that I had put aside a couple years ago. I had the privilege of attending a three-day intensive writing course with him, which brought to the forefront all that I needed to see and move through. This experience helped me recognize the blockages that were keeping me a prisoner to my emotions.

The author had prepared exercises of breathwork, meditation, and visualizations. He helped us push through our blockages around writing that were connected to inner core beliefs. He authentically and honestly guided people. He gave us all the tools and resources needed to be successful, not only in our writing process, but in our lives. He was someone who did not promise anything but delivered with integrity, something that I respect greatly. At another blockage, God sent me another sign. He sent me someone who entered my life during a moment when I needed it, someone who guided me to my healing without even knowing it. When one door closes, a window always opens.

Let me tell you, writing a book in English has been one of the biggest challenges I have ever taken on. Although I had done work on my self-worth, writing brought on many moments of despair and doubt. At times I believed I couldn't do it, and I wondered if anyone would care to hear my story. There was a quote that kept running through my mind, a sentence said by this author during our intensive days with him that kept travelling with me in these darkest moments: "Writing is easy but doubting ourselves is exhausting." Indeed, I was exhausted from doubting myself. I found a new and deep form of self-love in self-discipline. Oh, and let me tell you, writing a book takes self-discipline! I had to give myself permission to make some sacrifices. I had far too many weekends and months where I needed to sacrifice time with my family.

At forty-three years old, I finally allowed myself to be me and to do something for myself. I pushed through my inner core beliefs and conditioning in hopes that I could inspire my children to always pursue their dreams and follow their hearts. I am blessed to have a husband who has been my rock since day one. I am grateful for his loving support and for always believing in me even when I didn't believe in myself.

During the writing process, I faced some pieces of my life while I was writing that needed to be revisited so I could heal. As I mentioned earlier, the healing journey is an ongoing journey, and a commitment I made to myself many years ago to unveil any layer of trauma and pain for myself, for my children, for the people I work with.

## Journeying within the journey: Surrendering to the revelation of spirit using the power of psychedelics

A few years ago, I met an amazing woman named Dawn, a PhD educator who became my close friend and colleague. She is an educator who works exclusively with physicians struggling in the workplace. She was referred to me through a mutual friend to experience Reiki. Dawn had been experiencing burnout and was exploring different modalities as part of her own self-care plan. We had a few amazing energy healing sessions, and I created some tailored meditations for her.

For several months I did not hear from her, until our paths crossed again at a workshop. We reconnected, had lunch that day, and talked for what seemed like hours after the workshop. We maintained a close connection that grew naturally and organically into a close friendship. We spoke frequently and exchanged notes on different somatic healing practices and supported each other personally as we were both broadening our scope of practice. It was Dawn who encouraged me to get my trauma certificate. Dawn had an interest in learning Reiki and studied Level I with me.

Dawn became connected to Dimensions Health Centres, which focuses on using psychedelics to work with people experiencing post-traumatic stress disorder, anxiety, depression, end–of–life care, and trauma. Dawn's role was to create retreats for physicians and healthcare workers experiencing burnout and compassion fatigue. As part of her learning curve, she was training to become a cannabis therapist through Daniel McQueen, the director of medicinal mindfulness in Boulder, Colorado.

As part of her credentialing, she needed to practice, and asked if I would volunteer to be a guinea pig. I was intrigued yet skeptical. I had occasionally smoked marijuana recreationally in my twenties, but it was certainly not something I had continued using or incorporated in my life. Using psychedelics to address trauma and mental well-being was completely new to me. It sounded scary. The idea of ingesting any type of drug where I could potentially lose control or be taken to places that I did not want to go to, given my past, did not seem very appealing. However, over the next few months Dawn educated me on psychedelic therapy while I conducted my own research.

The word "psychedelic" derives from "psyche" (life, spirit, soul), which means "to breathe," and "delic," which means "to manifest, reveal, and make visible." So, psychedelics manifest the soul and make the spirit visible. As part of her cannabis credentialing, Dawn had experienced cannabis, and her journeys were deeply healing. The word "journey" is commonly used in describing a psychedelic experience. Cannabis is not traditionally known as a psychedelic experience but using cannabis therapeutically and not recreationally can be.

According to recent studies, the tetrahydrocannabinol in Cannabis is three times stronger than it was twenty years ago.[1] That said, Cannabis when used therapeutically is much safer, psychologically and physically speaking, than more familiar psychedelics such as ayahuasca or psilocybin. Apparently when used skilfully, cannabis can mimic the experiences of other psychedelics. The healing effects, which include releasing intense emotions, somatic release, and traumatic memory recall, are sometimes indistinguishable from MDMA (methylenedioxymethamphetamine, commonly called ecstasy) and other psychedelics.*

Cannabis has been described as a safe and sacred medicinal tool that supports us in turning inward, in resolving tensions stored deep within the body, in tracking inner sensations, and in releasing

[1] McQueen 2021

traumas from the nervous system. Using cannabis therapeutically is very different from using cannabis to get high and numb out. I liked the idea that one could use cannabis to turn inward and park the conscious mind, and in doing so safely explore and release trauma. Dawn talked about surrendering to the experience, meaning not resisting or paying attention to the inner critic or skeptic that may emerge. I had done a lot of inner work prior to working with cannabis, and I think that helped tremendously. I knew how to recognize that inner critic, acknowledge it, and then ignore it.

In a conversation, Dawn shared that successful journeys pay attention to what is called set, setting, and skill/integration. "Set" refers to your mindset going into a journey. Do you trust the medicine? Do you trust the person that will be holding space for you? Essentially, do you feel safe with what you are doing and who you are with? Trust is key to feeling safe and relaxed in the experience. If you do not feel safe, then the ego will not relax and will become preoccupied with making sure you are emotionally and physically on guard, defending against letting go into the experience. It reminded me of what it was like falling asleep when I was younger. It was harder to surrender to sleep when my father was on edge, or when I felt extreme tension in the house. We can relax into slumber if we feel safe, but if we do not, we sleep with one eye open and fight it. It is like that with psychedelics. If you don't feel safe, then it is hard to relax into the experience.

The more Dawn and I spoke, the more interested I became. I knew she would keep me safe. I trusted that I had done enough work that I would not become overwhelmed, and if I did, I was protected by Dawn. Although Dawn reassured me that cannabis was safe, she made me go through a safety protocol to make sure I had no contraindications. Do you have a history of . . .? Do you take . . .? This procedure reassured me that there were standards before screening and ensured that someone was okay to do this. No matter how good something is reported to be, there are always exceptions.

"Setting" refers to when and where one would be ingesting the plant medicine. Again, do you feel safe? We agreed that I would set a date and time I would not be preoccupied with the kids, or feel consciously or unconsciously rushed or pressured, which could be of concern. I was familiar with Dawn's house, and she indicated we would have space and privacy in her basement apartment. I felt comfortable, like I did not have to fall asleep with one eye open.

## More Than A Fleeting Moment

Finally, Dawn talked about the importance of integration afterwards. What did you learn, and how are you going to integrate that into your life? The flame of momentary enlightenment needs to be tended to if this is to become real change, otherwise it will dissolve back into unconsciousness and into just a fleeting memory of becoming high. The discussion resonated with me, and it is what I believe in. There is integration needed to embody our experiences, and the inner work is needed.

Psychedelic experiences need to be assisted and integrated to process, resolving what comes out somatically (in the body), but also emotionally and mentally. Even though I have never liked to lose control of my body, I understood that having journeys with cannabis was not for the high, but for the light that would shine on what I needed to heal, taking me to the epicentre of my wounds. My protective ego would be momentarily sidelined so I could gain a different perspective on my experiences with my family and, in particular, my father.

I trusted my friend, and I was ready to experience this approach. I reminded myself that plant medicine has been around since the beginning of time. It has been used throughout the centuries to explore and repair what we may not be able to access in a day-to-day conscious state. I was ready to welcome the plant medicine in my body with grace and gratitude. I was ready to explore the wisdom of our forefathers. I was ready to see what emerged.

Set, setting, and integration. I was ready.

## The journey

It began with a small ceremony where I thanked the plant medicine and its wisdom. I was ready to surrender without expectations. Dawn turned on a playlist of music and I began inhaling a cannabis blend of sativa, indica, and hybrid. When I felt I'd had enough, I put on an eye mask, turned up the music, and lay down. Dawn did a body-scan exercise to help me relax, and I was well on my way before she finished.

My first experience was intense. It began with a warm presence on my right side that never left. It was like I was being protected and guided. I was being reminded of how loved I was. It was intensely grounding. I travelled to the most beautiful places in the Universe. For a while, I was surrounded by beautiful colours, sights, and sounds. There was no fear. It was like I was being prepared to explore some challenging moments, because when the music shifted, so did my experience.

I was being shown windows of my past, but I could peek from a safe distance. Suddenly, one window opened and I found myself in a room that I did not recognize, but I recognized myself. I was a newborn baby, less than six months old. I was in a crib dressed in a blue sleeper with a white collar I did not recognize. My father came over, picked me up from the crib, and slapped my little bum. I found myself gasping for air. I saw his face, his look. I could feel how angry he was at me. His eyes were fireballs filled with resentment, and there it was: the feeling of being unwanted. I never heard anything from him that would confirm that, but I always felt unwanted by my father. I always questioned if I had been found in garbage bins as a child. I could read it in his eyes. I was a burden, a responsibility he did not want, and yet I was this tiny defenseless little baby. I was hurt, angry, confused, and disappointed. Why did he not love me? What could I have possibly done? I was just a tiny baby.

The warm presence that seemed to be blanketing me and coming from my right suddenly took me out of that dark, threatening room, and I travelled into a beautiful field of flowers. Some I hadn't seen before, and the colours were magically radiant. It was like I had never experienced colour before.

There was a voice telling me, "It was never about me; it has always been about my father. I am loved, and I am love. That is who I am." Throughout the journey, I kept being shown moments from my past. The comforting light was always with me, and I felt like a witness observing from a safe distance. Each time, I saw my father for who he was: a man consumed with anger and pain. Although I had done work in the past and I cognitively knew it was never about me, this was somehow different. It was like I had gotten it for the first time. I truly got it, and I embodied that truth. It was not about me. It was about a man wrestling with his own demons. It was not about my worthiness; it was about his lack of capacity to give me what I needed. I was always enough.

There it was: the message I needed to hear. It was never about me, it was about my father. I don't know his story, I don't know or hold the whys of his life, but I know now that it has nothing to do with me. He was not able to give me the love I deserved and needed. But I am loved, and who I am is pure love. That is who we truly are.

When the journey was over I sat with Dawn for a long time, sharing my tears, talking about what I had seen and experienced in trying to make sense of it. It felt profound, and somehow I felt freed. I felt like I had truly let go.

**Tying The Loose Ends**

I was surprised by the detail in my journey. How could I experience the past so vividly? It seemed so real, yet how could I possibly recall those memories from being so young? While my memories were still fresh, I called my older sister. Anais was six years older than me. I did not tell her I had smoked cannabis. I told her I had a strange dream and wanted to ask her some questions. I described the room, the crib, and my outfit. Anais was shocked. She confirmed that what I experienced was my room when I was first born. She confirmed that the crib was in the corner, and that I had a blue sleeper with little flowers on it. Anais recalled the blue sleeper because she had chosen it with my mother before I was born.

Everyone thought I was going to be a boy, hence why they picked out a blue sleeper. I shared how I felt unwanted by our father. Anais confirmed that he was hoping for a boy, but when I was born he was so disappointed that he did not have a girl name chosen. Ahh . . . things were making sense. My relationship with my father was torturous for both of us. He never wanted another girl. And certainly not a girl child who would spend her life defying him, talking back, asking questions, and challenging his authority. I decided from an early age I was never going to surrender to him. I wanted to be seen, heard, and loved, but he wanted to forget my existence.

My journey with plant medicine helped me turn an important corner. I emerged with a deep feeling of serenity and peace toward my father. There was nothing wrong with me. How could there be? I was nothing but love when I was born. My father's struggles got projected on to me. He could not give me the love I deserved and needed because he couldn't give it to himself. When I read these words to myself, they seem like common sense, but they don't do justice to what feels like a profound shift in myself that I attribute to plant medicine. Somehow, this medicine helped me deeply embody this realization. My cognitive ruminations about not being enough still occur occasionally, and when they do bubble up, I am able to quickly reconnect with that profound feeling of love to remind me that I am and always was enough.

When we get in touch with who we are, even if it is a glimpse each time, we dip into ourselves. We see and experience the world with a renewed lens. When we understand that we all have some level of trauma, needs that went unmet as a child, from adaptations we made to survive to perceptions of the world around us, we find ourselves in the breakthrough of finding our true essence. We can change the narrative of our story.

## Leaves of One Tree

Trauma is multifaceted and exists within the different realities of people's experiences on this planet. I also learned during my studies on trauma that socioeconomic status plays a role in the impact of trauma and on the experiences that we each have, collectively as communities and individually. For example, a mother of a Black child may have to worry about her child in ways that I, being white with white children, will never be able to understand. The Black mother may pass on traumas that white mothers like myself simply can't understand.

We have varying experiences in this one world. For example, I have never had to worry about explaining to my teenage son that wearing a hoodie at night could potentially be dangerous and life-threatening. Something like this may be inconceivable for me, but a very sad and unbearable reality for others.

As humans, we all have the same basic needs, which are to be heard, to be seen, to be accepted, and to be validated. Our experiences of how these basic needs have gone unmet are what make up our trauma, although our experiences of trauma may differ according to our story, social conditioning, and position in life. The need to have these basic needs met is a point of connection for all of us, I believe.

As I shared with you at the very beginning of Part II, my self-worth for the longest time was attached to a post-secondary diploma. I sat in my office so many times in front of people with different titles, degrees, and money, well-respected and honoured by society, who struggled with the same voice I faced, "You are not good enough," for the same need to be seen and heard.

We all are connected in this way, as we are connected to Mother Earth, the environment. As spiritual leader, poet, and peace activist Thich Nhat Hanh shares, "We are all leaves of one tree. We are all waves of one sea." Just like the ocean, each ripple has a different size or shape, but it still belongs to the ocean. If we could only look in our souls and energy instead of stopping at the body, we would understand that what we perceive as the truth is what Deepak Chopra refers to as "magical lies," which means that "what we perceive as the so-called truth is a mere perception." Our perception is based on our different stories, wounds, core beliefs, and conditioning. We may have different circumstances and beliefs, but our differences are to be honoured and cherished, not condemned or erased. Then can we finally and fully connect with the unity of our humanness because that is who we truly are. Our true essence is love.

The most important act of love is towards yourself. No one else has the power to change our lives—we do! The healing journey is not an easy road. There are so many bumps, falls, and turns along the way. You need to break free from the familiar patterns to walk on an unknown path to unpack and unlearn years of conditioning and limiting beliefs. It requires courage and honest introspection and self-inquiry. It is not an easy process, but I hope if you are reading this book and contemplating or reflecting on your life, you will commit yourself to finding your answers and your healing path. It is so much easier to numb the pain or stay unconscious, this is true. But remember, you are unique in this world. Your uniqueness is a gift! You are a light that this world needs to shine bright. Be curious like a child who always ventures. Take the leap and jump into the adventure of finding who you truly are. Unleash your full potential. Undertake the adventure to unlearn all you learned and unpack all the conditioning that made you believe you were not enough, that it was too late to try. You cannot fail at being who you are because there is no one like you!

Believe that if you connect with your mind, body, and soul, and create harmony within you physically, mentally, emotionally, and spiritually, then you can tap into your inner intelligence, your inner pharmacy, and experience the wellness that this life has to offer you. Wholeness is who we are. Our happiness depends only on us, no one else. It is our birthright to be joyful and happy. Our magic is an inside job, no one can unleash it for us.

You can heal your wounds and become the best version of yourself. You are the superhero in your life story.

# Acknowledgements

With gratitude to:

Neil Strauss, for inspiring me and helping me find the confidence to write my book. Your intensive writing class profoundly inspired me.

To all the beautiful authors I met there: your support has been deeply appreciated.

Deep gratitude for you, Michael Caputo, the English Mathematician. Thank you for teaching me the techniques of the English language. I am grateful for all the insights you provided to this project.

To my dear Louisa Nunes, from offering your feedback to your kind support: thank you for your continuous cheerleading and your insights. I am grateful for you.

To my friend Dr. Dawn Martin, for believing in me and opening your world to me. Thank you for being my Louise.

To my soul sisters: you are my lighthouse. I love you more than words can express. Our love and bond of so many years is untouchable by the physical space between us. Our friendship is a blessing in my life. Thank you for loving me for who I am.

My friend and spiritual teacher, Rui Manuel: your guidance and friendship is so important in my life.

To my close circle of friends in Canada and many other places of the world, the ones I trust and who unconditionally love me: I am grateful for each one of you. I love you all.

My dear clients: for sharing and trusting your journeys with me, and for the enthusiastic anticipation for this book. Thank you for your continuous support and cheerleading. I am deeply grateful for each one of you.

To my Chopra family and fellow instructors: you are a gift. So much gratitude for you all.

To my spiritual teachers, Nelson Mandela, Mother Teresa, Louise Hay, Dr. Deepak Chopra, Dr. Wayne Dyer, Oprah Winfrey, Brené Brown, who inspired me to heal and continue to be a source of inspiration in my journey: thank you for paving the way.

# About the Author

É milie Macas is an integrative Reiki teacher with a particular focus on emotional healing, as she holds a trauma counselling certification. Émilie is a Chopra Meditation teacher, a mindfulness educator, an author, a public speaker, and a mental health and wellness advocate.

Émilie has worked for decades treating some of society's most vulnerable, attending to children, people struggling with burnout, stress, and lack of general well-being. Émilie teaches self-care, alignment, and healing through embracing vulnerability, adopting a spirit of raw truthfulness, releasing fears, and finding acceptance for the things that cannot be changed. She helps people find their way back to their genuine passion, vitality, and *joie de vivre* through honest introspection and dedication.

To connect with Émilie visit www.emiliemacas.ca

Printed in Great Britain
by Amazon

18113442R00140